THE BEDFORD SERIES I

Manifest Destiny and American Territorial Expansion

A Brief History with Documents

Amy S. Greenberg

Pennsylvania State University

BEDFORD / ST. MARTIN'S   Boston ◆ New York

For Bedford/St. Martin's

Publisher for History: Mary Dougherty
Executive Editor for History: William J. Lombardo
Director of Development for History: Jane Knetzger
Senior Editor: Heidi L. Hood
Developmental Editor: Debra Michals
Production Supervisor: Andrew Ensor
Executive Marketing Manager: Jenna Bookin Barry
Editorial Assistant: Laura Kintz
Project Management: Books By Design, Inc.
Cartography: Mapping Specialists, Ltd.
Permissions Manager: Kalina K. Ingham
Text Designer: Claire Seng-Niemoeller
Cover Designer: Marine Miller
Cover Art: Currier & Ives, "Westward the Course of Empire Takes Its Way,"
    1868, lithograph. © Bettmann/Corbis.
Composition: Achorn International, Inc.
Printing and Binding: RR Donnelley and Sons

President: Joan E. Feinberg
Editorial Director: Denise B. Wydra
Director of Marketing: Karen R. Soeltz
Director of Production: Susan W. Brown
Associate Director, Editorial Production: Elise S. Kaiser
Manager, Publishing Services: Andrea Cava

Library of Congress Control Number: 2011936844

Manufactured in the United States of America.

6   5   4
f   e

For information, write: Bedford/St. Martin's, 75 Arlington Street, Boston, MA 02116
(617-399-4000)

ISBN: 978-0-312-60048-8

Distributed outside North America by PALGRAVE MACMILLAN
Houndmills, Basingstoke, Hampshire RG21 6XS

Foreword

The Bedford Series in History and Culture is designed so that readers can study the past as historians do.

The historian's first task is finding the evidence. Documents, letters, memoirs, interviews, pictures, movies, novels, or poems can provide facts and clues. Then the historian questions and compares the sources. There is more to do than in a courtroom, for hearsay evidence is welcome, and the historian is usually looking for answers beyond act and motive. Different views of an event may be as important as a single verdict. How a story is told may yield as much information as what it says.

Along the way the historian seeks help from other historians and perhaps from specialists in other disciplines. Finally, it is time to write, to decide on an interpretation and how to arrange the evidence for readers.

Each book in this series contains an important historical document or group of documents, each document a witness from the past and open to interpretation in different ways. The documents are combined with some element of historical narrative — an introduction or a biographical essay, for example — that provides students with an analysis of the primary source material and important background information about the world in which it was produced.

Each book in the series focuses on a specific topic within a specific historical period. Each provides a basis for lively thought and discussion about several aspects of the topic and the historian's role. Each is short enough (and inexpensive enough) to be a reasonable one-week assignment in a college course. Whether as classroom or personal reading, each book in the series provides firsthand experience of the challenge — and fun — of discovering, recreating, and interpreting the past.

Lynn Hunt
David W. Blight
Bonnie G. Smith
Natalie Zemon Davis
Ernest R. May

Preface

It can be easy to take the physical shape of the United States for granted. But the expansion of thirteen colonies into a continental empire in less than a century was the result of a great deal of luck; ceaseless labor; brutal, racially based warfare against Indians and Mexicans; and an extremely potent ideology known as Manifest Destiny that cast western expansion as natural and predetermined. It is this history that provides the central topics addressed in this volume—ones that all Americans should seek to understand, in part because their legacy lives on today.

This documentary history of Manifest Destiny offers an accessible and engaging approach to the history of American territorial expansion by placing nineteenth-century political events in their social contexts and presenting carefully selected primary sources that allow students to draw their own conclusions about why territorial expansion evolved the way it did. Unlike most other works on Manifest Destiny and western expansion, this volume emphasizes the social and cultural roots of the aggressive expansionism of the 1840s, highlights ongoing struggles with Indian peoples throughout the nineteenth century, includes a strong transnational perspective beyond the U.S.-Mexican War, and illuminates the dramatic but thwarted expansionist efforts of the 1850s, particularly filibustering and attempts to acquire Cuba. Beyond this, it also reveals evolving ideas of American influence abroad and charts the changing meaning of *destiny* from Puritan settlement through the embrace of overseas territories in 1898. Thus, this volume provides students with a unique perspective on the historical roots of modern American foreign policy and situates the United States in a hemispheric context. In the past decade, the scholarship of the United States has become increasingly internationalized in focus. Instructors looking to introduce a transnational focus to a class might note that few topics more clearly connect the United States with the rest of the world than Manifest Destiny.

This volume is divided into two main parts. The first part offers a brief history of America's territorial expansion from the colonial period through the Spanish-American War (1898). This introduction emphasizes the roles that changing notions of race, gender, religion, and class played in promoting Manifest Destiny and integrates Native Americans into the history of the transfer of North American lands between European powers.

The introduction contrasts expansionism in the early American republic with that in the decades following 1830 and grounds Manifest Destiny in its economic and social contexts. The rapid economic and social transformations in the 1830s and 1840s helped propel Manifest Destiny to the forefront of political debate, turning a vague sense of America's mission into a politically potent call to arms. The beginning of industrialization in the Northeast, the rise of evangelical religion, increased immigration from Europe, the hardening of class divisions and decreased mobility for workingmen, and the beginnings of the woman's rights movement created an ideal environment for the flourishing of an ideology based on the supposed racial and gender superiority of white, American-born men.

The introduction also illuminates the sectional consequences of expansion. Manifest Destiny and slavery were closely linked by both supporters and opponents of territorial expansion. Nothing did more to divide the North and South in the 1850s than conflict over the status of slavery in new territories, and students will learn why Manifest Destiny and national unity proved incompatible. The introduction concludes with an examination of the fate of territorial expansion in the late nineteenth century, charting the eclipse of territorial expansion in favor of commercial expansion in the three decades after the Civil War, as well as the reasons for the rebirth of aggressive expansionism and the drive for foreign colonies in 1898.

The second part of this volume comprises forty-seven documents, organized to complement the main themes of the introductory essay. These texts were chosen to reflect the diversity of viewpoints on Manifest Destiny from both within and outside the nation's boundaries. Classic texts and important speeches on Manifest Destiny by key political figures are represented, but so too are reflections by ordinary Americans, Indian people, and Latin Americans. Political cartoons and song lyrics provide a sense of the popular culture of Manifest Destiny, while artistic representations of western expansion offer another frame of reference. The wide diversity of sources here invites readers to draw their own conclusions about the meanings and implications of Manifest

Destiny in the Western Hemisphere. To facilitate students' understanding, each document features a headnote illuminating its specific context, while footnotes explain any obscure words or references in the text itself.

Additional pedagogical aids designed to encourage student learning are included in this volume. Five maps in the introduction chart the history of American territorial expansion from the colonial era through the annexation of Hawaii and reveal the extent of Native American control of U.S. land in the nineteenth century. The chronology following the documents will help place the readings within the often complex history of territorial expansionism, while a list of questions for consideration will aid class discussion of the material. A selected annotated bibliography, organized by topic, offers students a starting point for delving more deeply into the issues discussed, and an index makes it easy for them to locate key names, topics, and events in the book.

A NOTE ABOUT THE TEXT

Although many groups are entitled to call themselves Americans, in the interest of clarity this volume follows nineteenth-century convention by reserving the term for residents of the United States. I refer to the indigenous peoples of North America whenever possible by the tribal names most familiar to readers, but collectively either as Native Americans, Indians, or Indian people(s), with preference given to the last.

ACKNOWLEDGMENTS

It has gradually become obvious to me that nothing decent is written (at least not on my part) without a great deal of help and feedback from others. The volume you hold in your hands owes its existence to many generous people. Jonathan Earle, University of Kansas; Andrew Isenberg, Temple University; Robert E. May, Purdue University; John Putnam, San Diego State University; Charles Woodrow Sanders, Kansas State University; and Jeffrey Shepherd, University of Texas at El Paso, submitted careful, detailed, and thoughtful reviews of an early draft of this manuscript. I thank them for pushing my analysis in fruitful directions and for saving me from both interpretive and factual errors. Much of this material was tested out on my amenable students at Penn State in seminar and lecture courses over the past fifteen years. Their responses have informed every aspect of this project. Fellow scholars of Manifest

Destiny and the culture and politics of the early American Republic have widened my horizons with their work and in many cases provided concrete assistance in the creation of this book.

Thanks also to my able research assistant, Elizabeth Anderson; to the staff of the Penn State History department; and to the Richards Civil War Era Center at Penn State, which provided a generous grant in support of this project. The team assembled by Bedford/St. Martin's has been a pleasure to work with from start to finish. Bill Lombardo originally encouraged me to write this volume, Debra Michals was an excellent developmental editor, and both Heidi Hood and Jennifer Jovin answered questions quickly and efficiently. Andrea Cava supervised the production of the book for Bedford/St. Martin's, and Nancy Benjamin at Books By Design faultlessly managed the day-to-day production work. Penn State's library staff, particularly in Interlibrary Loan and the Rare Books Room, proved crucial to the completion of the volume. My greatest thanks go to my family—Rich, Jackson, and Violet—and to the Greenbergs of Santa Barbara and Santa Monica, California. I dedicate this book to my father, whose thoughts on the matters addressed in this volume have greatly influenced my own.

Amy S. Greenberg

Contents

Maps

PART ONE

Introduction:
The "Free Development" of a
North American Empire

*Other nations have . . . the avowed object of thwarting our policy and
hampering our power, limiting our greatness and checking the fulfillment of our manifest destiny to overspread the continent allotted by
Providence for the free development of our yearly multiplying millions.*
— *United States Democratic Review*, July 1845

The present-day borders of the United States are the result of neither
luck nor accident. In 1776 Indian peoples and European imperial powers controlled the vast expanses of the North American continent, while
thirteen rebellious British colonies hugged the Atlantic coast. Just
eighty years later, the United States embraced a continental empire. This
astounding transformation was the result of territorial expansion, an
ongoing process that involved ceaseless labor on the part of politicians
and settlers, treaties with European nation-states and Indian peoples,
and the forced dislocation of Native Americans from their land. Territorial expansion began almost as soon as English settlers arrived on
American soil and continued until the "closing" of the frontier in 1890
and the subsequent annexation of America's Pacific territories in 1898.

The long process of American territorial expansion was both facili-
tated and justified by a mid-nineteenth-century ideology (or national
vision) known as Manifest Destiny. In the 1840s, Manifest Destiny
accelerated western settlement and provided a rationale for continued

continental expansion. It cast western expansion as natural and pre-determined and legitimated a policy of brutal, racially based warfare against both Indians and Mexicans. Starting in the late 1830s, American politicians asserted, and many citizens believed, that God had divinely ordained the United States to grow and spread across the continent. The course of American empire, supporters insisted, was both obvious (manifest) and inexorable (destined). Not everyone believed that the United States had a manifest destiny, of course, but by the 1840s the majority of Americans seemed to agree that the growth of their nation to the Pacific Ocean was natural and inevitable. They turned to war to achieve that goal in 1846. In the 1850s, with a continental empire firmly in place, the idea of Manifest Destiny became both more expansive and more ambiguous. Some southerners coveted the Caribbean as an extension of their slaveholding empire, while expansionist northerners looked longingly at Hawaii and Canada. Many Democratic politicians and journalists, hoping to hold the two halves of their party together, suggested that America's destiny might encompass the annexation of the entire Western Hemisphere.[1]

The fracturing of the national consensus over the future of the country's Manifest Destiny was directly related to the rise of the sectionalism that territorial expansion helped unleash. When northerners and southerners refused to compromise over the status of slavery in newly won territories, the only thing still manifest was the inevitability of a civil war. After the war, Manifest Destiny went into eclipse. For thirty years, Americans remembered Manifest Destiny as an antebellum relic, and nationalists pushed to control international trade rather than foreign land. But the ideology experienced a rebirth in 1898 when supporters of war with Spain claimed that America's Manifest Destiny had imperial dimensions.

This volume focuses on Manifest Destiny and territorial expansion in the crucial decades before the Civil War, when the United States took its continental form. It explores when and why Manifest Destiny emerged, how Manifest Destiny differed from the territorial expansion of the early decades of the Republic, what arguments opponents marshaled against it, and how the relationship between Manifest Destiny and slavery proved the undoing of both Manifest Destiny and national unity. It also examines the ideological origins of Manifest Destiny and the reinterpretation and renewal of Manifest Destiny in the late nineteenth century.

Manifest Destiny was a political and intellectual creation of the 1840s, but its impact on the larger course of American territorial expansion has

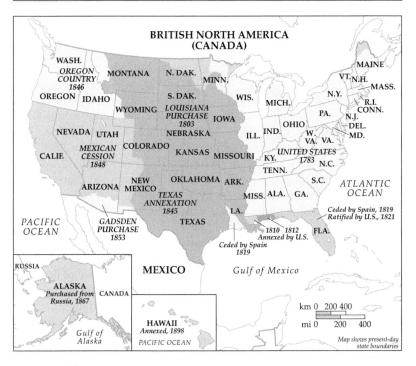

Map 1. *U.S. Territorial Expansion*
This map represents U.S. territorial expansion in relationship to the claims of other European powers.

been profound. As a reflection of a deep-seated sense of superiority, as a rallying call, and as a smoke screen for immoral and sometimes illegal actions by both state and citizens, Manifest Destiny became one of the most influential ideologies in American history. It justified the relentless displacement of Native Americans from the colonial era forward; a war of aggression against Mexico in 1846 that stripped it of half its land; attacks on Canada, Mexico, Cuba, and Central America by private American mercenaries known as filibusters; and military action to gain overseas colonies in the late nineteenth century, despite the fact that the United States, once itself a colony, defined its identity in opposition to European empire. Without Manifest Destiny, the territorial expansion of the United States from a strip of Atlantic coast colonies to a continental empire in less than a century would have been, literally, unthinkable (Map 1).

THE IDEOLOGICAL ORIGINS OF
MANIFEST DESTINY

All nations are defined by their shared myths, but only the United States had Manifest Destiny. While Manifest Destiny was a creation of the nineteenth century, the concept of American exceptionalism (the belief that the United States occupies a special place among the countries of the world) is actually older than the nation itself. Zealous English Protestants brought their faith in God's will with them to New England. The seventeenth-century Protestant dissenters known as Puritans asserted that their arrival in the New World—and their survival there against all odds—was proof of God's approval (Document 1). They envisioned their experimental settlement as a "citty upon a hill," a beacon of light for less blessed people elsewhere that would prove the superiority not only of Protestantism over Catholicism but also of strict Puritanism over less rigorous practices of Protestantism (Document 2).

British colonists were fiercely ambitious about the future of their settlements. The colonial charters of Massachusetts, Connecticut, Georgia, North Carolina, and Virginia laid claim to land extending to the Pacific, ignoring other European powers on the continent as well as the Native American residents of that land. Colonists began to move west almost as soon as they arrived, violating British treaties with resident Indian tribes. By the American Revolution, colonial settlement extended more than two hundred miles from the coast, and more than 100,000 Americans lived west of the Appalachian Mountains.

That there was something special in the rapid growth of the young nation appeared clear to early national leaders. Although no one at the time of the Revolution envisioned a single American nation spanning three thousand miles, John Adams and Benjamin Franklin took note of the rapid population growth in the colonies (Document 3). The fact that the white population of the United States doubled between 1770 and 1790 was cause for celebration among nationalists who believed that the nation's physical increase would help it compete with the European powers that threatened on every side. As president, Thomas Jefferson suggested that the United States might become an "empire of liberty," expanding its beneficial sway far to the west.[2] Even in the early years of the Republic, many Americans accepted the continued expansion of the nation as both natural and inevitable, particularly given the so-called inferior racial composition, religious practices, and social systems of other North American residents, from Indian peoples to the French and Spanish Catholics who claimed territory south and west of British settlement.

The American people saw their triumph over the powerful British Empire during the Revolution as providential: It was so remarkable that it could only be attributed to the will of God. The novelty of the political ideology of the Republic, which was based on the informed consent of a wide body of citizens, also provided secular support to the sacred notion that Americans were a people set apart. Eighteenth-century American geography textbooks justified western expansion in racial terms. They explained to children that the "savages" of the continent would necessarily make way for the industrious European settlers of the United States, and they looked forward to the day when American citizens would colonize areas west of the Mississippi River (Document 6).

In short, virtually everything about their young nation—from its admirable origins in New England religious settlements through its astounding population growth, miraculous victory over the great British Empire, racial and religious superiority over other residents of the continent, and novel form of government—proved to Americans that their nation, above all others, was unique and marked by God for a special destiny. This shared belief in American exceptionalism lay at the heart of the ideology of Manifest Destiny.

At the close of the eighteenth century, the victors in the American Revolution were smug in their belief that the political rights, social relations, Protestant religion, and economic system of the young United States were superior to others and could be beneficially bestowed on everyone else. It would be several more decades before journalists, politicians, and average Americans began to insist that the advantages of American settlement *should* be bestowed on the world. That, they claimed, was Manifest Destiny.

TERRITORIAL EXPANSION IN THE EARLY REPUBLIC

There was little that was natural or predestined about the process of territorial expansion. Even before the Northwest Ordinance of 1787 provided for the settlement and governance of federal land west of the Appalachians, settlers illegally occupied the region and expected their new government to provide protection from resident Indian people, something the British had often been unwilling to do (Document 4). But tribes in the Old Northwest (the area northwest of the Ohio River and east of the Mississippi) refused to vacate their land, repeatedly rejecting treaties they considered illegitimate (Document 5). After years of warfare and the continued failure of treaty negotiations with a confederacy of Northwest tribes, including Iroquois, Hurons, Shawnees, and Delawares, President George Washington directed U.S. forces to subdue them militarily. Defeat at the Battle of Fallen Timbers in 1794 drove Indian people in the Old Northwest to cede two-thirds of Ohio and a portion of Indiana in the Treaty of Greenville (1795).

President Thomas Jefferson took a dramatic step toward his empire of liberty when he purchased the vast trans-Mississippi region (828,000 square miles) from France in 1803 for $15 million. Jefferson had no explicit constitutional authority to purchase land on behalf of the United States. But his concerns about the potential threat posed by the presence of the French on the Mississippi, as well as his desire for the Gulf of Mexico port of New Orleans and the rich farmland of Louisiana—already home to sizable American settlements—overshadowed his constitutional scruples (Document 8).

Jefferson's opponents in the Federalist party objected to the purchase not only on partisan grounds but also because they imagined a host of dangers resulting from territorial growth. According to this view, when a nation shared a language, values, and experiences, it prospered. Extended empires with diverse populations, such as ancient Rome or modern Britain, fractured and collapsed. Federalists asked how the United States could develop its existing resources if it continued to focus on extending its boundaries. Both Federalists and Jefferson's Democratic-Republicans were dismissive of the "inferior" Catholic and racially mixed inhabitants of the trans-Mississippi West, but Federalists worried that those inhabitants would prove impossible to integrate into America's political, economic, and social systems. Democracy might collapse under the weight of such potentially corruptible voters (Document 7).

Democratic-Republicans, who believed that democracy and economic progress would result from the widespread acquisition and distribution of land, shared few of these reservations. Jefferson was confident that "no constitution was ever before so well calculated as ours for extensive empire & self government."[3] The blessings of the American way of life could easily be extended, and the more territory the United States controlled, the less likely it would be that foreign powers would threaten America. Britain, in particular, loomed large in the fears of Democratic-Republicans.

This division between supporters and opponents of expansionism would continue to animate partisan politics. Until the late 1850s, Democrats continued to champion expansionism in aggressive terms, and their political opponents repeated warnings that growth would lead to internal weakness and national collapse.

The Louisiana Purchase ultimately doubled the size of the United States and set a precedent for presidential action in the interests of expansion. But equally significant was Jefferson's recognition that the purchase did not guarantee U.S. sovereignty. The exact boundaries of the Louisiana Purchase were hardly clear in 1803. The United States believed that they extended to Texas and portions of New Mexico. Spain claimed that the purchase covered only a small strip of land west of the Mississippi. And Britain openly questioned the legality of the purchase. By directing Meriwether Lewis and William Clark to explore the Pacific Northwest in 1804–1806, Jefferson laid claim to this disputed area. Thus, far from being manifest, America's territorial destiny was still up for grabs in the early nineteenth century.[4]

Increasing numbers of pioneers would make their way to the newly discovered Oregon Country in the coming decades, but immediately following the Louisiana Purchase, it was the areas adjacent to the settled portions of the United States that appealed most to land-hungry citizens and Democratic politicians. On the southern border of Georgia lay Spanish Florida. To the north of an ill-defined border lay British Canada, full of former Loyalists who had fled the American colonies during and after the Revolution. Given the lack of political representation Canadians enjoyed relative to Americans, many New Englanders in particular believed that Canada was ripe for revolution and annexation. In the Old Northwest lay a powerful confederation of Native American tribes under the leadership of Tecumseh, a Shawnee who refused to sign the Treaty of Greenville in 1795 (Document 9). Americans viewed all three areas as distinct threats to the survival of their young nation.

When the United States declared war against Britain in 1812, expansionists in the North and South grabbed what appeared to be a perfect opportunity to increase their security and further their dominion. Their hopes were thwarted when attempted American invasions of Canada were rebuffed at the border. General Andrew Jackson held Spain responsible for a British-led attack out of Pensacola on an American fort in Mobile Bay and used the pretext to invade Spanish Florida. But he was forced to withdraw to protect New Orleans from British assault. The War of 1812 ended with the United States' territorial boundaries with other European powers unchanged, although victories over Native American tribes in the West and South dramatically increased the amount of land available for U.S. settlement. The death of Tecumseh and destruction of his confederacy in 1813 opened up land from what is now Indiana to Wisconsin to U.S. expansion, while Jackson's victory over the powerful Creek tribe in the Southeast enabled Americans to settle half of Alabama and part of southern Georgia.

In 1818 Jackson again invaded Spanish Florida, under the pretense of protecting American settlers there from runaway slaves harbored by the Seminoles. In the eighteenth century, Spain had been the most powerful empire in the New World, but revolutionary movements across Latin America, combined with financial difficulties at home, had left the Spanish with little power to protect their North American interests. Spain was forced to cede Florida to the United States in the 1819 Adams-Onís, or Transcontinental, Treaty. Spain also surrendered its claim to Oregon in return for the United States surrendering its claim to Texas.[5] Another important treaty, between the United States and Great Britain, established joint control of the Oregon Country beginning in 1818.

The Adams-Onís Treaty was celebrated in large part because it increased the security of the United States from interference by European powers. In 1823 President James Monroe took another step in that direction when he presented an ambitious statement of U.S. foreign policy in his annual message to Congress. The Monroe Doctrine, as it would later be known, divided the globe into two spheres of influence and warned Europeans that the Western Hemisphere was outside their jurisdiction. This doctrine codified a policy of the Jefferson and Madison administrations that the United States would not tolerate a weak European power transferring an American colonial holding to a stronger European power. It also offered the first hemispheric vision of U.S. hegemony. Little was made of Monroe's statement in 1823, but in the late nineteenth and twentieth centuries, expansionists would use the Monroe Doctrine to justify hemispheric domination in the name of national security.

Territorial expansion in the early Republic was impressive in its scope and accomplishments, but it was largely haphazard. While a few committed nationalists contemplated the annexation of Canada and dreamed of an American settlement on the Pacific, there was no national consensus before the 1830s regarding the future of the nation's boundaries. Many Americans, particularly in the Northeast, thought the country was already large enough. Military engagements were, at least on the surface, defensive in character and driven by security concerns. Early expansionism lacked both the national coordination and the ambition it would later exhibit, but it set a number of precedents that would shape the dramatic events of the coming decades.

FACTORS DRIVING EARLY EXPANSIONISM

Early territorial expansion was driven by security concerns and by population growth. Americans had large families in the eighteenth and nineteenth centuries, and the mortality rate was relatively low compared to that of Europe. That fact, plus a constant influx of European immigrants, led to a growth rate that astonished both European and American observers. Between 1790 and 1830, the U.S. population more than tripled to nearly thirteen million people. Settlers moved west because there was no room for new farms in the increasingly dense settlements of the East.

The United States was also an overwhelmingly rural nation in the first half of the nineteenth century, and the individual ownership of family farms was a cherished ideal to which most Americans aspired (Document 14). Settlers in British North America and their offspring were unusually mobile compared to populations elsewhere and were willing to move repeatedly for better land and increased opportunity. Federal land policies also encouraged the settlement of new territory by offering newly surveyed land at low prices—although often with minimum purchase requirements that left most of the territory in the hands of "land speculators," individuals who bought and sold land for the purpose of profit rather than settlement.

Speculation became a major factor in western expansion. In the boom years after the War of 1812, a frenzy of speculative land fever transformed the trans-Appalachian West. Settlers in the Old Northwest wrote home about the "Ohio feever" and "Missouri and Illinois feever" that drew them ever farther west. Immense profits through land speculation appeared within the reach of ordinary farmers. In 1815 alone, 831,000 acres of Ohio land were transferred to private ownership. By 1820 there was virtually no public land left for sale in Ohio, and settlers set their sights on Illinois, Missouri, and Indiana.[6]

Those who could not afford to buy land simply occupied it. These squatters, as they were known, repeatedly infringed on the property rights of Indian people. The federal government sometimes evicted squatters from Indian land, particularly when they interfered with treaty negotiations or U.S. land sales (Document 4). But for the most part, the federal government turned a blind eye to squatters (Document 15).

EXPANSIONISM AND INDIAN PEOPLE

Although the history of America's territorial expansion is almost always narrated in terms of the shifting ownership of land between European nations and the United States, it is important to remember that the Indian peoples of North America had original claims to the land they occupied (Map 2). The fact that Native Americans generally rejected the concept of individual landownership does not invalidate this. In the eighteenth century, all European powers laid claim to territory over which effective control was clearly in the hands of Indian tribes, and Native Americans were often the dominant powers in areas where the young United States hoped to expand. During much of the nineteenth century, the United States was unable to settle what it considered its "own" territories because they were controlled by Indians. The history of U.S. expansionism is on the one hand the tale of treaties and wars between European powers, and on the other hand a far messier story of individual conflicts between settlers and Indian people, punctuated by bloody Indian wars, from first contact until almost the close of the nineteenth century. All of these conflicts were eventually resolved in favor of white Americans (Documents 5, 9, 10, 11, 12, 15, and 46).[7]

The inability or unwillingness of government forces to rein in American settlers indicates the degree to which whites consistently disavowed Native American claims to their own land. Indians were seen as a nuisance or a threat, but rarely as holding legal and legitimate title to land desired by whites. In part this was due to the different views that Indians and whites had about proper land use. The Indian peoples of the Old Northwest, for instance, reserved extensive shared tracts for hunting. But in the minds of white Americans, if land could be cultivated and was not, it was being wasted. Enlightenment theories of land use that predated the United States supported this position and suggested that by leaving land fallow, Indians actually gave up their claims to that land. So even when federal law was against them, squatters often felt justified in occupying Indian land.

Nor was it only individual settlers who ignored Native Americans' claims. Time and again, both state and federal governments proceeded

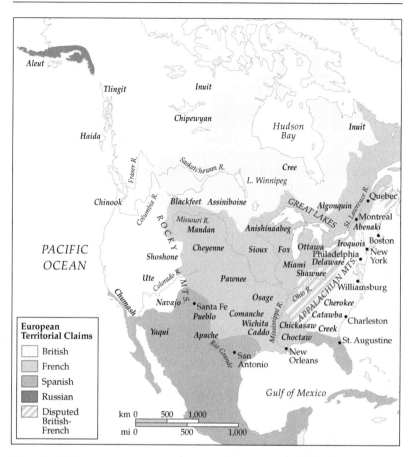

Map 2. *Indian Nations and European Territorial Claims, ca. 1750*
European territorial claims in the eighteenth century overlapped with those of
Indian peoples who occupied and in many cases controlled the territory.

as though those claims were invalid (Document 10). The federal government is the only entity with the constitutional power to negotiate with
Indian tribes. Still, in the eighteenth and nineteenth centuries, states
and territories encouraged squatters to invade Indian land and occasionally surveyed and sold such land. At the federal level, the government
repeatedly tried to coerce treaties from captured Indian people and
bribed minority interests within tribes who lacked the authority to sign
treaties. Although officials recognized that treaties signed under these
circumstances did not represent the best interests of the tribes, they

often proceeded as if those treaties were legitimate. Similarly, promises made in treaties, particularly those stating that the United States would not encroach further on Indian land, were rarely honored.

Just after the Revolution, the United States coerced treaties from the Iroquois League of Six Nations and from the Delaware, Huron, and Miami tribes, while failing to consult with other tribes occupying land that the United States surveyed for white settlement (Map 3). When tribes in the Old Northwest refused to cede their land in the 1790s, President Washington ordered military action against them. President Jefferson never consulted the tribes of the Mississippi Valley when he purchased their land from France, nor did France consult them when selling it, despite the fact that France had treaties with many of them acknowledging tribal authority over their own land. Although the United States agreed to honor France's treaties with resident tribes, Indian peoples were not treated as partners in the negotiations.

On the contrary, the fact that Indians rather than Europeans occupied a region was seen as legitimating U.S. expansion into that territory. White people in Europe and America shared the belief that there was a "natural" racial hierarchy that placed whites above nonwhites due to the alleged superiority of white "civilization." Because "civilization" was really a code word for whiteness, Native Americans (and later the racially mixed residents of Mexico) could not be "civilized." Settlers used this reasoning to justify taking their land.

The conflation of civilization and landownership also shaped the federal government's foreign policy decisions. One reason for the scant Spanish presence in Florida in the second decade of the nineteenth century was Seminole dominance in the colony. Yet Americans used the absence of Spanish authority as justification for seizing Florida, which was passed from Spain to the United States via the Adams-Onís Treaty—and not via a treaty between the Seminoles and the United States.

White Americans refused to acknowledge Native American landownership or to honor their own legally negotiated treaties with Indian peoples even when Native Americans closely conformed to white ideals of civilization. That Indian people could never become "civilized" because they could never become white was proven in the tragic case of the Cherokees in Georgia during the 1820s. In every way possible, the Cherokees adopted the social, political, economic, and cultural norms of their white neighbors. Yet they were forced off their land after the Indian Removal Act of 1830 authorized the expulsion of eastern tribes

Map 3. *Indian Land Cessions to 1810*
The young United States devoted its energy to acquiring Indian land beyond
the Ohio River through both treaties and the military defeat of resident tribes.

to west of the Mississippi. Their sustained protests reveal the extent to which they assimilated white ways (Document 12), but the fact that they were not white ultimately cost them their land. The blunt assertion by white Americans that they were entitled to the land of nonwhite peoples simply by virtue of their race was perhaps the most important early precedent for the bloody expansionism of the 1840s.

SOCIAL TRANSFORMATIONS AND THE BIRTH OF AGGRESSIVE EXPANSIONISM

At the close of the 1820s, expansionism began heating up. One of the favorite metaphors of expansionists was that of territories dropping into America's lap like fruit falling from a tree. But this passive vision of expansion would give way to a more martial, or military, vision, and the conviction by many that violence—against Indian peoples and European neighbors—might be a necessary and appropriate means for the nation to expand.

This transformation was grounded in a host of changes. An evangelical religious movement known as the Second Great Awakening swept the nation in the 1820s and convinced American Protestants that God wanted them to spread the word of his salvation. Religiously "awakened" Americans believed that the spiritual conversion of the entire nation would usher in a millennium of peace on earth. A vivid strain of anti-Catholicism had always energized Protestantism, but the Second Great Awakening exacerbated the American tendency to view the Catholic nations to the south and west of their country as a distinct challenge to their religion and security (Document 13).

At the same time, a cultural movement imported from Europe known as romanticism inspired American philosophers, writers, and artists to embrace emotion and strive for self-perfection. The nation's greatest intellectuals, from novelist James Fenimore Cooper to philosopher Ralph Waldo Emerson, encouraged Americans to reject European precedent and instead look both inward and to the great American frontier for inspiration. Their elevated rhetoric seemed to foster the idea that the United States' growth could be boundless (Document 19).

A combination of economic and social transformations in the 1830s and 1840s helped propel territorial expansion to the forefront of political debate, turning a vague sense of America's mission into a politically potent ideal celebrated by politician and newspaper editor alike. The rise of a market economy and the beginning of industrialization in the

Northeast, combined with mass immigration from Europe, led to a hardening of class divisions and decreased mobility for workingmen. At the same time, women began to lobby for increased rights, which further challenged traditional notions of men's and women's roles. These factors provided an ideal environment for the flowering of Manifest Destiny, an ideology that justified expansionism by pointing to the supposed racial and gender superiority of white, native-born men.

The first clear journalistic expression of America's Manifest Destiny appeared in 1839 in the *United States Democratic Review*, a journal closely affiliated with the Democratic party (Document 17). Although attributed to journal editor John L. O'Sullivan, it may have been one of his writers, Jane McManus Storm Cazneau (who wrote under the pen name Cora Montgomery), who coined the term. The attribution is disputed, but the deeply gendered character of Manifest Destiny certainly encouraged generations of scholars to assume that a man, rather than a woman, came up with the idea.[8] In a now famous 1845 essay promoting the annexation of Texas (Document 25), the *Democratic Review* proclaimed that foreign powers were thwarting "the fulfillment of our manifest destiny to overspread the continent allotted by Providence for the free development of our yearly multiplying millions." It asserted that God had preordained expansion across the continent, that expansion was the natural result of the population growth of the United States, and that meddling foreign powers such as Britain and France needed to be checked in order for America to achieve God's will. The following year, the *Democratic Review* made a similar claim about America's Manifest Destiny to take all of the jointly controlled Oregon Country from Britain.

These assertions appeared outlandish to objective observers. British politicians, Mexican journalists, and members of the opposition Whig party, among others, wondered how it was that the United States could suddenly claim "a right for a new chapter in the law of nations" (Document 26). Why should the United States be justified in taking land from its neighbors?

But to many Americans, Manifest Destiny appeared as common sense. The phrase became immediately popular. In reality, there was nothing predestined about Manifest Destiny. It was a self-serving ideology that achieved a variety of purposes, few of which were noble. Land speculation had helped drive expansion since the colonial era. In the first decades of the nineteenth century, speculators had bought up vast tracts of midwestern land with the expectation that it would quickly increase in value. In the 1830s and 1840s, speculators set their sights farther afield. Many of the most active proponents of Manifest Destiny (including John L. O'Sullivan and Cora Montgomery) owned foreign investments in Mexico, the Caribbean, and Central America that would vastly increase in value under the U.S. flag.

Expansionism was also a winning issue with voters, particularly in the South and the trans-Appalachian West. Many residents of what were then "western" states, including Tennessee, Kentucky, Missouri, Ohio, and Illinois, were the products of a western migration from states in the East. They speculated in western land, understood that western migration would increase the value of their property, and might move even farther if conditions proved auspicious. Southern slave owners also stood to profit from the increased value of their slaves when new areas appropriate for staple-crop agriculture opened to settlement, creating yet another market for slaves. Anglophobia was rife among both groups. Westerners feared British encroachment, and southerners dreaded the influence of British antislavery activists. Manifest Destiny promised to limit British power in North America.[9] Politicians in these regions employed the language of Manifest Destiny to get elected and reelected.

It was no coincidence that America's "destiny" was usually commensurate with advancing its economic interests, particularly control of international trade via the valuable harbors of the Pacific and Gulf coasts. Commercial interests in East Coast cities embraced Manifest Destiny because they wanted access to lucrative shipping routes to Asia. Businessmen in New Orleans saw immense profits in an American Yucatán, Cuba, and Central America. Manifest Destiny papered over base instincts, casting land hunger and greed as God's plan.

But Manifest Destiny also was a matter of faith to millions of white Americans who believed themselves racially and culturally superior to nonwhites. Although territorial expansion in the early Republic had not proceeded peacefully, the expansionism of the 1840s—encapsulated and supported by the ideology of Manifest Destiny—was newly aggressive, clearly grounded in racism, and driven by the conviction that all nonwhite peoples must necessarily bend to the will of whites. Until the 1830s, Americans justified taking land from "savages" because they were not farming and "improving" their land by constructing permanent structures on it. But after the ethnic expulsion of the civilized Cherokees—a tribe that both farmed and improved their land—in the 1830s, race and not civilization became the determining factor in this equation. Increasing numbers of "Anglo-Saxon"[10] Americans believed their claims to North America to be superior to those of any racially "impure" peoples.

Transformations in race relations within the United States in the 1830s were central to the intensifying drive to expand its boundaries. The last vestiges of colonial slavery did not disappear in the northern states until the 1840s. Gradual emancipation in the North turned slavery into a purely sectional phenomenon, putting southerners on the defensive about their "peculiar institution," but also leading to social unrest north of the Mason-Dixon Line. The newly elevated status of northern freedmen, along with the increasing size of free black urban communities, led to an upsurge in northern racism in the 1830s and 1840s.

One reason for this was that white workingmen in the North faced increased competition from free African Americans and surging numbers of immigrants drawn to the United States by declining conditions in Europe. Between 1840 and 1860, almost four and a half million European immigrants arrived in the United States, the largest influx in U.S. history relative to the total population of the country. Many of those immigrants were Catholics from Ireland and Germany, resulting in a notable increase in anti-Catholicism and fears among Protestants of an attempted European-led Catholic takeover of the U.S. political system (Document 13). The working conditions of laboring men also declined with the beginnings of the industrial revolution and the devaluing of many traditional artisanal skills.

Workingmen faced new challenges to their cultural values along with decreasing wages in the 1830s and 1840s. An emerging middle class embraced temperance and church attendance. They rejected the heavy drinking and rowdy male camaraderie that was once the norm in artisan workshops of the early Republic and among some immigrant groups. By the 1830s, these behaviors were seen by many in the middle class as uncouth.

The emerging middle class also began to idealize women for their supposed moral superiority to men. A new ideology of domesticity insisted that women and men were essentially different and suited to different spheres of influence. Men's realm was the public world of work and politics; women's was the home. What was new was the elevation of women, by middle-class women and men, to a place of equality with men in religion and family matters, as well as the assertion by women that their domestic virtue entitled them to exert their influence beyond the home into society. This empowerment of women through the ideology of domesticity helped spark the first woman's rights movement in the 1840s.

All these changes left workingmen—who based their self-worth on their physical strength, traditional labor skills, and dominance over both women and nonwhites—on the defensive. By raising women to a level of equality with men in the home, domesticity threatened to remove one of the few prerogatives available to men whose working lives were increasingly unrewarding. Manifest Destiny promised workingmen upward mobility and an escape from declining working conditions through landownership on the frontier. In reality, few urban workers moved to the frontier. Virtually all western settlers were farmers who had already found at least moderate success working the land. It was simply too expensive to purchase land and equipment, and survive until the first harvest, for laborers or poor farmers to start a western farm.[11]

Manifest Destiny obscured this painful truth. Proponents of Manifest Destiny repeatedly claimed that cheap land, beautiful women, and a better life were free for the taking by the man willing and able to fight for them. Travel writers, musicians, and politicians made the same promises about land, love, and a generally easier life in California, Texas, Mexico, and even Central America (Documents 18, 24, 32, and 39).

Southerners were as enthusiastic as northern workingmen about aggressive expansionism. Mass immigration to the North left the South outnumbered in the House of Representatives, where representation is based on population. This worried southerners concerned about slavery's future. After the Missouri Compromise of 1820 prohibited slavery in the territories north of latitude 36°30′ (with the exception of the new state of Missouri), southerners began to look south for new territory. Expansion could bring additional slave states into the Union, strengthening the power of the South. It also promised an opportunity for nonslaveholding white yeoman farmers, who made up the bulk of the southern population, to gain slaves and land. This, too, would strengthen the institution of slavery.

Aggressive or violent expansionism in the heyday of Manifest Destiny was also encouraged by scientific racism. In order to "prove" that Anglo-Saxons were destined to dominate lesser races, leading scientists of the antebellum era, many from the South, posited theories of racial difference that expanded on earlier ideas of a racial hierarchy. This logic was used to justify slavery, but it also promoted Manifest Destiny. Contemporary race theory similarly suggested that through the sexual union of white men and Latin American women, Mexico might be whitened, since Anglo-Saxon characteristics would overpower nonwhite characteristics in the next generation. In the literature of Manifest Destiny, Mexican women were repeatedly represented as sexually desirable, hardworking, and, unlike the newly empowered women of the United States, easily dominated. Race theory promised that what

Senator Sam Houston of Texas called "annexation" between white U.S. soldiers and Mexican women, would result in Anglo-Saxon hegemony in newly annexed Mexican territories (Document 32).

Aggressive territorial expansion offered men the promise of asserting their martial virtues; dominating supposed racial inferiors; and — by dint of their physical strength and courage — winning fertile land of their own, docile women, and an empire for the United States. In a period when workingmen, Democrats, and slaveholders were quick to fight, or to threaten to fight, upon the slightest provocation, Manifest Destiny offered rewards (Document 27). Not surprisingly, aggressive expansionism was supported by men who embraced physical domination by individuals and nations.

Manifest Destiny appealed to a wide spectrum of Americans and crossed party, gender, class, and racial lines. Although racism underlay demands to annex foreign territories, African American men were not immune to the idea that they could "best develop" their "manhood" abroad, in either Central America or Liberia (Document 40). Cuban exiles in the United States were among the strongest supporters of the annexation of Cuba in the 1840s and 1850s for financial and ideological reasons (Document 34).[12] Even middle-class female proponents of the emerging ideology of domesticity made use of Manifest Destiny. By arguing that their domestic virtues were needed to civilize the frontier, women claimed increased power in the public realm (Document 29).

Indeed it was the flexibility of Manifest Destiny that made it such a potent idea. The most violent expressions of Manifest Destiny in the 1840s and 1850s were driven primarily by pressure from southerners and from white workingmen in the North. But before the nation's "destiny" devolved into a war of aggression against Mexico in 1846, a wide variety of Americans imagined that territorial expansion would improve their lives.

OPPOSING VOICES

Topping the list of opponents of America's territorial expansion were people who stood to lose, particularly Native Americans. They protested in various ways, from unification movements (Document 9) to armed uprisings (Document 11), and from congressional petitions (Document 12) to speaking engagements intended to raise awareness among white people of their plight (Document 46). Residents of Latin America and the Caribbean fought Manifest Destiny through diplomatic negotiation and war; they published trenchant critiques of what they recognized as American avarice (Documents 33 and 41). The British, who also stood to lose power as the United States expanded, employed diplomacy to fight Manifest Destiny.

There was substantial opposition to the ideology within the United States as well. One of the era's two major political parties, the Whigs, was openly ambivalent about territorial expansion. Whigs believed that America's future greatness lay in the development of resources within its existing boundaries, not in the annexation of more territory. They lobbied for the growth of the manufacturing sector and improvements in transportation to bring already settled areas of the country in closer contact. They feared that western expansion would undermine the interests of New England, the seat of Whig power. And, like the Federalists before them, they feared that growth would lead to division by making the nation too large and unmanageable (Document 22). Many people in New England, particularly middle-class women and men, opposed Indian removal in the 1830s and the U.S.-Mexican War in the 1840s on the grounds that the "civilized tribes" and Mexicans deserved their land. They argued that both actions were immoral.

Although concepts of racial hierarchy promoted and legitimated Manifest Destiny, they also left some Americans uneasy about the annexation of land to the south. Southern slaveholders generally supported the annexation of slave-filled Texas in 1845 (Document 21). But more than a few opposed the war with Mexico and the acquisition of more Mexican territory on the grounds that the racially mixed residents of those areas were unfit to become Americans (Document 31). Opponents of slavery protested vociferously against any new annexation of land that might increase the power of the South. Abolitionists (antislavery advocates) viewed the annexation of Texas and the U.S.-Mexican War as proof that the South exerted inordinate control over the federal government (Document 28).

Most of the Americans who opposed Manifest Destiny and territorial expansion in the 1840s and 1850s believed wholeheartedly in American exceptionalism. They were just as convinced that the United States was a special nation, chosen by God to exert a beneficial influence abroad, as were supporters of Manifest Destiny. Many of them might be described as "restrained expansionists." They supported missionary work abroad and pushed for the United States' commercial expansion. They hoped to spread American ideology but opposed aggression, both by individuals and by nations (Document 26). They believed that American influence could best be exerted through the control of trade and the dissemination of Protestant Christianity, not by the annexation of land. Most Whigs fell into this category.

ANDREW JACKSON AND THE MARCH TO THE SOUTHWEST

While the Whig party generally opposed aggressive expansionism, their opponents, the Democrats, embraced it. The Democratic party was born in the 1820s. Closely aligned with urban workingmen in the North and yeoman farmers in the South, it was the perfect vehicle to promote an expansionist agenda. Democrats looked back to Thomas Jefferson for inspiration and asserted that the future of the Republic was tied to physical growth. They believed that the widespread distribution of land and a weak central government would best preserve American democracy and ensure individual prosperity.

Andrew Jackson, the first president from the trans-Appalachian West, garnered fame fighting the Creeks and Seminoles during the second decade of the 1800s. He won the presidency in 1828 in part by promising to remove Indian peoples from valuable land east of the Mississippi River. Jackson used all available resources, from bribes to the brute force of the U.S. Army, to remove the Cherokees, Creeks, Choctaws, Chickasaws, and Seminoles to Indian Territory (what is now Oklahoma) during the 1830s (Documents 10 and 12). Thousands died on the brutal journey, which became known as the Trail of Tears. Indian removal opened up extensive regions to white settlement in what is now the Southeast. It also set the important precedent of a president employing the U.S. Army in the explicit service of territorial expansion.

Ironically, while Manifest Destiny displaced Indian peoples by moving them west, it advanced along Native American trade routes. Although Mexico became independent from Spain in 1821, Mexican control over the northern half of its territory was at best sporadic. The vast Com⁻ che tribe—20,000 strong in 1840—dominated what is today the ⸍ can Southwest, controlling trade and demanding payment frᵣ and European settlers alike and inhibiting Spanish settᵗ¹ ern slaveholders, enticed by cheap land, poured iⁿ⸍ in the 1820s and 1830s. By 1828 it was apparerᵗ that these settlers were a problem (Documᴄ there were 35,000 Anglos in Texas and only

Texans (Tejanos). In 1836 the Anglo settlers rebelled against Mexico and, with the help of hundreds of recruits from the American South, won a brief war for independence. Although Texas's independence seemed to provide evidence to Americans that "Anglo-Saxon" dominance was inevitable, in reality the Comanches and other tribes continued to exert significant control over the region.[13]

THE OVERLAND TRAIL

As southerners were revolutionizing Texas, thousands of northerners trekked by covered wagon to the Oregon Country, jointly controlled since 1818 by Britain and the United States. Starting in the late 1830s, Americans increasingly made the six-month trek to Oregon, despite the brutal terrain and weather conditions. By 1843, a thousand emigrants a year were departing Missouri on the Overland Trail. Most believed that the magnificently fertile soil they found in Oregon more than made up for the difficulties of the journey. Soon Americans outnumbered the British in the region, while increasing numbers of wagons headed south from the trail to Mexico's Alta California.

In 1846 twelve thousand members of a new religious sect set out by covered wagon from Illinois, seeking a land where they could escape persecution for their controversial doctrine of polygamy. Brigham Young and his Church of Jesus Christ of Latter-day Saints (Mormons) settled in the valley of the Great Salt Lake, on Mexican land that would soon be transferred to the United States at the close of the U.S.-Mexican War. In 1850 the settlement the Mormons called Deseret became part of the incorporated territory of Utah.

Travel writers extolled the virtues of Oregon and California, convinced that the United States would soon control those regions, and ordinary travelers expressed the opinion that America, seemingly more capable than other nations, would eventually claim all of the Pacific coast (Documents 16 and 18). A group of avid expansionists in the Democratic party who called themselves Young America (in opposition to "old" England) made Manifest Destiny their rallying cry (Document 19). They espoused the "reannexation" of both Oregon and Texas, territory they claimed had wrongfully been signed away in treaties with Britain in 1818 and 1819 (Document 21). Some also demanded the immediate annexation of Canada, Cuba, and the Mexican provinces of California, Sonora, and Nuevo Mexico on the grounds of Manifest Destiny. Soon, however, had a war on their hands.

ANNEXATION AND WAR WITH MEXICO

Texas became an independent republic in 1836. Both the president of Texas, Sam Houston, and his good friend U.S. president Andrew Jackson hoped to see the speedy annexation of Texas by the United States. But Mexico refused to recognize the independence of its former province. Congress, unwilling to go to war with Mexico and divided over the advisability of adding another slave state to the Union, sidestepped the Texas issue for eight years. In 1844 President John Tyler negotiated a secret treaty of annexation with Texas. After Democrat James K. Polk was elected president later that year on an explicitly expansionist platform, Congress admitted Texas as a U.S. state over the objections of Mexico (Document 23). Polk entered office intent on also acquiring California and prepared to fight a war to do so.

Polk, a Tennessee slaveholder, won northern support in his presidential bid by promising that the United States would take all of Oregon from the British. He quickly settled for half of that, dividing Oregon along the forty-ninth parallel and leaving British Columbia to the British. Polk was saving his fight for Mexico, a fact that infuriated many of his supporters in the North and ultimately led to a rift in the Democratic party between southern expansionists looking for new slave territories and northern "free-soil" Democrats who hoped to see a ban on slavery in new territories (Document 30).

As soon as negotiations with Britain over Oregon were complete, Polk turned his attention south. He ordered U.S. troops into an area between the Nueces River and the Rio Grande, a region that was claimed by both Mexico and Texas, openly antagonizing Mexico. A border clash was inevitable, and on April 25, 1846, Mexican forces killed sixteen U.S. soldiers. Although Texas's claim to the area was tenuous at best, when Polk learned that Mexican troops had fired on U.S. forces, he informed Congress that "American blood" had been shed on "American soil," and asked for a declaration of war. Members of the opposition Whig party in Congress, terrified of being branded unpatriotic, swallowed their scruples and endorsed a war they believed to be unjust.[14]

Sixteen months of combat followed, far longer than most Americans—convinced of their racial and military superiority—could have imagined. Although the U.S. Army won virtually every battle with Mexico, the war had the highest casualty rate of any American war then or since: one out of every ten American soldiers in Mexico lost their lives, the vast majority to disease. At least 25,000 Mexicans perished as well. This war introduced the U.S. Army to the now familiar experience of military occupation of a racially and linguistically foreign populace. U.S. soldiers committed atrocities in Mexico, including the rape and murder of civilians, which horrified not only the Mexicans but also the soldiers' own commanding officers and American civilians back home. At the same time, newspaper correspondents, who for the first time followed the troops into battle, turned war into entertainment by providing thrilling narratives and a cast of heroes to an enthralled reading public.

At the onset of the hostilities, the war was loudly and enthusiastically celebrated almost everywhere outside New England as proof of America's God-given mandate to spread over the continent. But by the summer of 1847, a growing antiwar movement began to question the direction that Manifest Destiny seemed to be taking. Some Americans wondered whether waging a war against a weaker neighbor was really part of God's plan and questioned the value of the new territories and the people who resided in them.

On August 8, 1846, President Polk requested $2 million from Congress to negotiate an end to the war. A Democratic congressman from Pennsylvania, David Wilmot, offered a proviso banning slavery from any territory gained from Mexico. The proviso passed in the House but not in the Senate, with voting falling along sectional rather than party lines. For the first time, the Democratic party split over the issue of slavery, with many northern Democrats making it clear that they would not condone the spread of slavery into territory that rightly belonged in the hands of free white men (Document 30).

Expansion and sectional harmony were proving incompatible. Antislavery Democrats in the North began to desert the party for the new Free-Soil party. The opposition Whig party, which opposed the war for reasons ranging from morality to self-interest, hoped to defuse the growing sectional division by calling for an immediate end to the war without taking any territory from Mexico (Document 31).

Still, success in Mexico inspired many Americans to broaden their horizons. A solid contingent of expansionist Democrats demanded the annexation of all of Mexico as the spoils of war. Between October 1847 and January 1848—with the United States occupying Mexico City but with no peace treaty in hand—avid expansionists gathered in mass meetings, calling for the immediate annexation of all of Mexico (Document 32).

Members of Polk's cabinet were divided over how much territory the United States should take from its defeated neighbor. Some wanted a limited settlement along the lines of the present-day boundary between the two countries. Others, including Polk, hoped for vastly more land (Document 27). A rogue diplomat named Nicholas Trist negotiated a limited settlement with Mexico *after* being recalled from his duties by Polk.[15]

The war officially ended in early 1848 with the signing of the Treaty of Guadalupe Hidalgo, transferring 500,000 square miles of Mexican land to the United States for $15 million. Mexico lost her provinces of Alta California and Nuevo Mexico, along with parts of Tamaulipas, Coahuila, and Sonora—land that would form the U.S. states of California, Nevada, and Utah, as well as parts of Texas, Arizona, New Mexico, Kansas, Oklahoma, and Colorado. Much of this land might have been gained from Mexico through negotiations, but the United States put far less energy into diplomacy than it might have. Manifest Destiny provided the justification for war that many white Americans welcomed. Most were so dismissive of Mexico and Mexicans that they believed it would be a simple matter of bullying the country out of California. In fact, Mexican soldiers fought tenaciously and won American respect on the battlefield. Mexico did not lose in 1848 because its people were weaker than Americans. Mexico lost because it was essentially fighting three wars at once: against the United States, against Indian tribes on the northern frontier, and against itself in a civil war between factions of the federal government.[16]

Although the Treaty of Guadalupe Hidalgo promised the new Mexican American residents of the United States full citizenship rights, racism and the unwillingness of local judges and juries to uphold the law in favor of Mexican Americans led to their political disenfranchisement. Many Mexican Americans unjustly lost their land to Anglo settlers.[17] For the United States, the war produced lasting Mexican enmity and opened a Pandora's box of sectional tensions over slavery in the new territories. The resulting sectional crisis was resolved with the deaths of more than 600,000 Americans in the Civil War.

With the Treaty of Guadalupe Hidalgo, the United States became a continental empire. In name at least, it was in sole possession of all the territory between the Atlantic and Pacific oceans. In fact, the nomadic societies of the Great Plains held title to much of this land through binding treaties with the United States and exerted physical control of vast stretches of the West. But to white observers, those claims were illegitimate. In 1851 the United States assigned territories to various Plains tribes to lessen the frequency of intertribal conflicts. Although the United States lacked the power to enforce compliance with the boundaries, the

1851 Treaty of Fort Laramie offered a tentative plan for the control of the plains. With European powers pushed to the periphery of the continent, America's Manifest Destiny was almost complete in the 1850s.

Or was it?

FILIBUSTERING: TAKING MATTERS INTO THEIR OWN HANDS

The vast territorial acquisitions resulting from the U.S.-Mexican War inflamed the desires of Democratic expansionists, who envisioned the United States encompassing Sonora, Mexico; Cuba; Canada; and lands even farther afield. They saw the successful conclusion of war with Mexico as legitimating a hemispheric destiny for America. On their own, some of these individuals planned, and occasionally executed, attacks on other nations. These adventurers were called filibusters, and they operated without the official sanction of any government, although often with the implied support of Democratic politicians.

Like less violent expansionists, filibusters were driven by a desire for opportunities abroad that seemed closed to them at home. The popular insurrections and revolutionary fervor that gripped Europe in 1848 were closely followed by the American press and proved inspirational to fledgling revolutionaries. Filibusters, like other true believers in Manifest Destiny, claimed that American political, social, and religious forms would improve the condition of residents of new territories. But they also coveted the fertile land, natural resources, and valuable ports of these potential acquisitions and hoped to gain money, love, and fame abroad (Document 39).

Filibustering didn't start with the U.S.-Mexican War. Former vice president Aaron Burr was arrested by U.S. authorities in 1807 on charges that he was planning on filibustering in Spanish Mexico. Spanish Florida and Mexican Texas were popular targets of American filibusters in the second decade of the 1800s, and Americans were involved in many of the independence movements that reduced Spain's once mighty New World empire to a pair of Caribbean islands by 1824. After attempts to annex Canada in the War of 1812 failed, it became one of the leading targets of filibusters through the 1830s. Canadian efforts at fighting ecclesiastical favoritism, high taxation rates, and the limited representation accorded them by Britain struck a sympathetic chord in the United States. Rhetoric supporting Canadian freedom was sometimes followed by failed invasions. Canada faded as a locus of filibustering attention in the 1840s after the boundary with the United States was resolved and the British granted Canada self-government. Mexican Texas, occupied primarily by Americans disgruntled with Mexican law, was the other major target of aggressive expansionists in the 1830s. Given that few of the soldiers fighting for independence in 1836 were permanent residents of Texas (most came from neighboring U.S. states), the Texas Revolution should also be considered an example of filibustering.

After 1848 the pace of filibustering plots accelerated dramatically. Mexico continued to be one of the most popular targets. Texans repeatedly crossed the Rio Grande, attempting to revolutionize the neighboring Mexican states of Tamaulipas and Coahuila. Only a few months after Mexico ceded control of California to the United States in the Treaty of Guadalupe Hidalgo, San Francisco newspapers reported the discovery of gold at a nearby lumber mill. California's population exploded as hopeful miners from around the globe poured into San Francisco. Not surprisingly, the reported great mineral wealth of Sonora attracted unwanted attention from gold miners, some of whom headed south as filibusters.

Central America also attracted expansionist attention. The gold rush provoked a sudden popular interest in Central America because the quickest and easiest route to the California goldfields from the East Coast was through Panama (then part of New Granada) or Nicaragua. Twenty thousand immigrants each year traveled by sea to California, the majority along the Nicaragua and Panama routes. In 1855, after the Panama Railway was completed at a cost of six thousand lives and $8 million, travel from New York to San Francisco could take just one month. By contrast, the more dangerous overland route generally took four months. A Nicaraguan canal proposed by Cornelius Vanderbilt would have made the "Isthmus route" even shorter. Thousands of Americans traveling through Nicaragua and Panama imagined the region Americanized (Document 41).

SECTIONALISM CHECKS MANIFEST DESTINY

In the late 1840s and 1850s, Democratic politicians frequently fell back on expansionism to unify a coalition fracturing over the question of slavery—although few were bold enough to publicly support filibusters operating in violation of U.S. and international law. President Polk set a standard for annexing land that future Democratic presidential candidates struggled to emulate. In his failed 1848 presidential bid against the Whig war hero Zachary Taylor, Michigan senator Lewis Cass did not hide his feelings about the issue. As Cass stated during the war with Mexico, "We want almost unlimited power of expansion." He advocated annexing the Yucatán when it declared its independence from Mexico in 1847. (Mexico settled its dispute with the province before the United States could take action, but not before many Americans left to help the rebels with the fighting.) He was a firm and lifelong supporter of the annexation of Cuba, since, he proclaimed, the Gulf of Mexico "should be ours."[18]

Many Americans agreed. The strategic location, fertility, and wealth (in sugar and slaves) of Cuba made it a natural target of filibusters. Narciso López, a Cuban expatriate living in the United States, gained international attention as he repeatedly tried to liberate the island from Spain in the late 1840s and early 1850s. With the help of American supporters (including *United States Democratic Review* editor John L. O'Sullivan) and followed by an American volunteer army, López seemed unstoppable. But in the summer of 1851, he and fifty-one American volunteers were captured in Cuba and put to death. This hardly dampened American ardor for the "Queen of the Antilles," and southerners and northern Democratic expansionists alike continued to target the slaveholding island throughout the decade (Document 35).

Although Zachary Taylor was elected president in 1848, he died soon after entering office. His vice president and successor, Millard Fillmore, worked to stop filibustering, most notably Narciso López's repeated attacks on Cuba. Yet even Fillmore's secretary of state, Massachusetts Whig Edward Everett, left the question of Cuba's destiny open. Everett asserted that the final destiny of Cuba was an American question, one that Europe had no voice in, and that the eventual annexation of the island "might be almost essential to our safety."[19] Fillmore, however, believed that America's future prosperity lay in the control of world trade, not the annexation of new territories.

New Hampshire Democrat Franklin Pierce, elected in 1852, made territorial expansion an explicit goal. He directed James Gadsden to bully or bribe Mexico into selling the United States enough land for a southern route for a transcontinental railroad. The Gadsden Purchase in December 1853 added an extra 45,535 square miles to the Southwest for $10 million. This brought Pierce singular success among Democratic presidents of the era, all of whom hoped to obtain land from Mexico after 1848.

His efforts to acquire Cuba through negotiations with Spain, however, were derailed by the public leak of the Ostend Manifesto. This document was drawn up by three of Pierce's European diplomats in 1854 after the minister to Spain, Pierre Soulé of Louisiana, bungled negotiations over Cuba. Soulé, along with the minister to Great Britain, James Buchanan, and the minister to France, John Y. Mason, declared in the manifesto that the United States should forcibly take Cuba if Spain refused to sell it (Document 36). The outcry against a document that seemed to license outright robbery—as a variation of Manifest Destiny—was overwhelming, and the administration was forced to repudiate it (Document 37).[20]

Aggressive expansionists became unhappy with Pierce after he ran afoul of the most famous filibuster of the era. Tennessee-born William Walker was a San Francisco newspaper editor who rose to national attention in the fall and winter of 1853 in an aborted attempt to capture land in Sonora and Baja California. In the fall of 1855, he seized control of Nicaragua, which was divided by civil war, and became the first commander in chief of the republic's army. The following July, he became president of Nicaragua. For a brief period that spring, the United States officially recognized Walker's Nicaragua, but the Pierce administration withdrew recognition after Walker made himself president. With Walker's political hold on the country in decline, the filibuster made a desperate attempt to gain the political support of the American South by reintroducing slavery into Nicaragua, where it had been illegal for thirty years (Document 42).

After losing a war in May 1857 to an army composed of Central Americans and the British, Walker returned to the United States and gathered funds for another invasion of Central America. In November 1857, he attempted to return to Nicaragua but was arrested en route and forcibly returned to the United States. Walker made one final foray to the region on the eve of the Civil War, meeting his death before a firing squad in Honduras in 1860.

Walker became one of the great cultural figures of the decade, a race hero who conquered a country by bravery and physical prowess. Pierce's refusal to support Walker cost him friends among aggressive expansionists who had celebrated the Gadsden Purchase and Ostend Manifesto. Pierce hesitated when faced with other opportunities as well. Special agent to the Dominican Republic William Cazneau (the husband of journalist Jane McManus Storm Cazneau [Cora Montgomery]) pushed him to annex that nation. Commodore Matthew Perry, who successfully "opened up" Japan to American trade in 1854 with the use of heavily fortified U.S. Navy vessels, encouraged Pierce to annex the Ryukyu Islands in the Pacific. Paralyzed by the mounting sectional crisis, the president ignored both suggestions.

At one point, Pierce had hoped to annex Hawaii, and his commissioner gained King Kamehameha's agreement to draft a treaty of annexation in 1854. But the movement stalled, in part because of fears of American aggression among Hawaiian residents. Despite the fact that U.S. business interests and many northern and western residents desperately wanted to annex the island chain, it remained independent until the turn of the twentieth century (Document 38).

The public backlash against the Ostend Manifesto did not prevent one of its authors, Pennsylvania Democrat James Buchanan, from winning the presidency in 1856 on an expansionist platform. Equating expansion and manliness, Buchanan argued, "Expansion is in future the policy of our country, and only cowards fear and oppose it." Lewis Cass, now Buchanan's secretary of state, was more enthusiastic, writing that the United States "requires more land, more territory upon which to settle, and just as fast as our interests and our destiny require additional territory in the North, or in the South, or on the Islands of the Ocean, I am for it."[21] Cass authorized the U.S. minister to Mexico to offer $15 million for Baja California and parts of Sonora and Chihuahua, an offer that was repeatedly rebuffed.

The Buchanan administration also tried to buy Cuba, but its hopes were thwarted by the exploding sectional conflict within the United States. Violence in Kansas between free-soil and slaveholding settlers, and the Supreme Court's 1857 *Dred Scott* decision that Congress had no power to prohibit slavery in federal territories and that people of African descent could never become citizens, drew attention away from expansion, while a financial panic that year devastated the manufacturing sector of the Northeast. When Democratic senator John Slidell of Louisiana introduced a bill in January 1859 allocating $30 million for the acquisition of Cuba, it was shot down by northern opponents.

That the United States did not forcibly take Cuba from Spain in the 1850s can be attributed to sectional discord. Were it not for the fact that the annexation of Cuba would bring another slave state into the Union, northerners would have happily taken the "Island gem" that many considered crucial to U.S. trade and security (Document 35).

Sectionalism first began to overshadow Manifest Destiny during the U.S.-Mexican War. While David Wilmot proposed in 1846 that all territory taken from Mexico remain free from slavery, James K. Polk angrily insisted that slavery was a "domestic" matter that had no place in discussions of the war. Privately, however, Polk's cabinet agreed that slavery would likely be allowed in the land taken from Mexico (Document 27). Divisions between North and South exploded in the contest over the issue, and northerners were no longer amenable to any territorial acquisition that might strengthen the South. The nation split along sectional lines over the Wilmot Proviso and remained split in the following years. Each attempt by southerners to gain new slave territory—and each debate over the status of slavery in the existing territories of the United States—exacerbated the division between North and South.

William Walker's Nicaragua initially held great appeal among both northerners and southerners, but by reintroducing slavery to Nicaragua in 1856, he deliberately aligned himself and Manifest Destiny with the South. Many southerners insisted along with Walker that expansion was necessary for slavery's survival. They threatened northerners with disunion if the North refused to support the annexation of slave territory (Document 43). Other southerners looked ahead to the looming sectional conflict and decided against further expansion in the 1850s in favor of saving resources for a possible war with the North (Document 44).

The Civil War (1861–1865) brought Manifest Destiny to a halt. From today's vantage point, the continental boundaries of the lower forty-eight states seem natural and predetermined. But in the 1850s, they were brand-new, and many people imagined that they were as temporary as the national borders after the American Revolution, the Louisiana Purchase, or the annexations of Florida, Texas, and Oregon. The possibility that Nicaragua, or Cuba, or even distant Hawaii could become a new state seemed more likely after the dramatic (if ill-gotten) gains of the 1840s than it had previously. Only in retrospect does the U.S.-Mexican War mark an end to antebellum territorial expansion. At the time, the war instead seemed to open the door to an ever larger United States.

AFTER THE CIVIL WAR: MANIFEST DESTINY REEVALUATED AND REDEEMED

In the era of Republican political power that followed the Civil War, commercial expansion appeared more appealing to most Americans than territorial expansion, marking an important shift away from Manifest Destiny. Expansionism took on a strictly commercial character in the late nineteenth century, with the Republican party proving an enthusiastic proponent of U.S. domination of international trade. They argued that commercial expansion was cheaper than annexation and saved the United States from incorporating the undesirable populations of foreign lands into the American polity. The U.S. Senate ratified William Seward's treaty to buy Alaska from Russia for $7.2 million in 1867 in spite of strong public objections to the expense, the seeming worthlessness of the land, and the Native American inhabitants of the region. Only three years later, the Senate rejected a treaty negotiated by President Ulysses S. Grant to annex the Dominican Republic, largely because of public unwillingness to incorporate the mostly nonwhite population into the Republic. In the 1840s, racism had encouraged Manifest Destiny. In the postbellum years, it proved a barrier against the policy.[22]

Many Democratic proponents of Manifest Destiny in the 1840s and 1850s had argued that nonwhite residents of newly annexed territories would blend into the multiplying white population of the United States. From the start of the nineteenth century, opponents of territorial expansion questioned this reasoning and doubted that American political, social, and religious practices could survive with a diverse population spread over great distances (Documents 7, 22, and 31).

After the ratification of the Fifteenth Amendment to the Constitution, prohibiting racial discrimination in voting, in 1870, northerners and southerners showed an unwillingness to recognize the political rights of nonwhite peoples. Northern Republicans withdrew their support from Reconstruction in the 1870s and shifted to healing the "rift" between white southerners and northerners by asserting a shared white supremacy. They allowed southern "redeemers" to disenfranchise and terrorize the black citizenry of the South.

The collapse of Reconstruction and ensuing attempts to find common ground between white northerners and southerners inhibited expansionism. It also led to the retrospective reimagining by white Americans of the Manifest Destiny of the 1840s and 1850s as a peaceful process of family settlement, a national movement in which the North and South were partners before the horrors of the Civil War (Document 45). The violence of Indian removal, the U.S.-Mexican War, and filibustering were forgotten. Instead, the myth of a "virgin West," empty and waiting for U.S. settlement, was propagated even as war against the Plains Indians heated up in the 1870s. While the United States proved more than willing to use military force to protect U.S. business interests, particularly in Latin America, few politicians showed much interest in annexing new territories.

Expansion abroad came to a standstill just as vast expanses of the U.S. interior were finally being settled. Advances in farming and building technology enabled white farmers to cultivate land on the plains previously considered uninhabitable, and liberal federal land policies led to a land rush in the last three decades of the century. In 1867, after a series of bloody wars, the Sioux, Cheyennes, Arapahos, Kiowas, and Comanches agreed to move to specific areas from which whites were prohibited (Map 4). Indians in California and Nevada were also settled on reservations after a decade or more of vicious treatment at the hands of white settlers (Document 46).

U.S. control of the plains remained far from certain in the first decade after the Civil War. The willingness of tribes in the northern and southern plains to submit to the reservation system was the result of the near extinction of the bison herds more than the power of the U.S. Army. After substantial gold deposits were discovered in Sioux territory in 1875, tens of thousands of miners descended on the region. The resulting Sioux War, in which George Armstrong Custer and 224 U.S. soldiers were killed at the Battle of Little Bighorn in June 1876, was the last major Indian war and marked the near-total subjugation of Indian peoples within the continental United States.[23] In 1890 the director of the U.S. Census Bureau observed that the continent was settled and the frontier was closed.

In the 1890s, Manifest Destiny and aggressive expansionism experienced a revival, driven by a familiar combination of racial, class, and gender concerns. Racial unrest at home in the form of segregation and lynching, along with the rise of the new doctrine of "social Darwinism,"[24] suggested to many white Americans that the continued survival of American Anglo-Saxons depended on the domination of other races at home and abroad. Industrialization and a financial depression starting in 1893 led to declining conditions for workers, while labor unrest caused concern among the management classes. Women's ongoing struggle for political rights also took on a new intensity at the close of the century.

As in the 1830s and 1840s, aggressive expansionism seemed to offer a solution to domestic problems and new opportunities for white men to assert their authority over those they considered their inferiors. With the West effectively settled, Americans looked abroad for a new frontier. The result was the open advocacy of gaining overseas territories as a means of strengthening American manhood and prevailing in the Darwinian struggle between the races that many white American intellectuals believed was under way (Document 47).

America's Manifest Destiny took on worldwide dimensions and an even more racist character than in its pre–Civil War incarnation. In 1898 the United States fought a war for territory against Spain, stripping it of

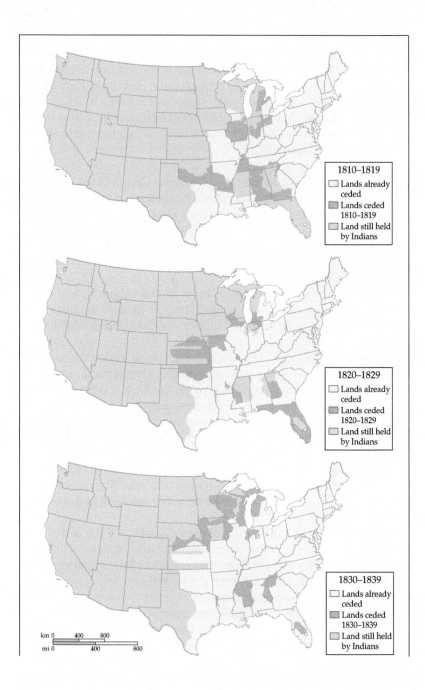

1810–1819
Lands already ceded
Lands ceded 1810–1819
Land still held by Indians

1820–1829
Lands already ceded
Lands ceded 1820–1829
Land still held by Indians

1830–1839
Lands already ceded
Lands ceded 1830–1839
Land still held by Indians

km 0   400   800
mi 0   400   800

34

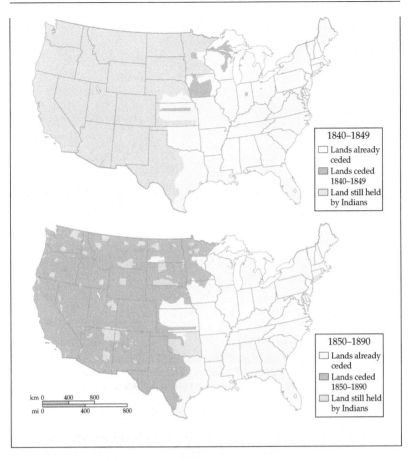

Map 4. *Indian Land Cessions, 1810–1890*
Between 1810 and 1849, the United States implemented a policy of removing all Indian tribes to west of the Mississippi River. In the second half of the nineteenth century, Indian possessions in the western half of the nation were reduced to a fraction of their former size, and Indian peoples were confined to reservations.

its remaining colonies. The following year, America began a war of colonial subordination against the Philippines that resulted in the deaths of hundreds of thousands of Filipinos. Although the annexation of the Philippines proved a cataclysmic disaster, the United States emerged from the wars in possession of Hawaii, Guam, and Puerto Rico (Map 5).[25]

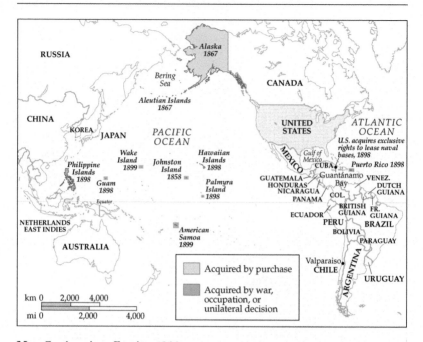

Map 5. *American Empire, 1900*
With the Spanish-American War of 1898 and the Philippine-American War of
1899, the United States gained a Pacific empire. Cuba was granted independence in 1898, although the United States retained control of Guantánamo Bay.

The rebirth of expansionism was made possible by an important shift
in ideas of empire and citizenship in the United States. Annexation in the
antebellum era was predicated on the idea that the newly incorporated
"Americans" would receive full political rights—although Mexican residents of the new Southwest after 1848 and Native Americans throughout the period found those promises maddeningly empty. But the rise
of social Darwinism and the racial upheaval of Reconstruction left white
Americans unwilling to acknowledge the political rights of nonwhites
at home or abroad. Colonial governance, decried as the cardinal sin of
European empire in pre-Revolutionary America, became law in the territories taken from Spain in 1898.

The fact that a nation that was born when colonists rebelled against
Britain could fight wars for colonies of its own is testimony to both the
ideological power and flexibility of Manifest Destiny. The perceived destiny of the United States dramatically shifted between 1840 and 1898,

from the incorporation of annexed peoples into the existing democratic structure to a global empire complete with colonies whose residents had limited political rights. But both were deemed manifest by supporters at the time.

The historical legacy of America's Manifest Destiny has been, at best, mixed. The United States gained an empire, but only after violently displacing Indian peoples and conducting a war for land against Mexico. Nor was there anything "free" about the development of the American empire. Sectionalism resulting from the status of slavery in new territories helped plunge the nation into civil war.

Yet ideas of American exceptionalism continue to live on. The ideological origins of Manifest Destiny—from the Puritan idea of the "citty upon a hill," to the astounding victory over the British in the Revolution, to the genius of the Constitution—still inspire admirers in the United States and around the globe. As long as many Americans continue to believe that the United States is uniquely situated to lead the rest of the world, Manifest Destiny will remain more than just a historical artifact.

NOTES

[1] Portions of this introduction are based on my *Manifest Manhood and the Antebellum American Empire* (New York: Cambridge University Press, 2005). Full documentation can be found in that work.

[2] Jefferson to George Rogers Clark, December 25, 1780, in *The Papers of Thomas Jefferson*, ed. Julian P. Boyd (Princeton, N.J.: Princeton University Press, 1951), 4:238.

[3] Jefferson to James Madison, April 27, 1809, in *The Papers of Thomas Jefferson: Retirement Series*, ed. J. Jefferson Looney (Princeton, N.J.: Princeton University Press, 2004), 1:169.

[4] Andrew Isenberg, "The Market Revolution in the Borderlands: George Champlin Sibley in Missouri and New Mexico, 1808–1826," *Journal of the Early Republic* 21, no. 3 (Autumn 2001): 445–65; David Weber, *The Spanish Frontier in North America* (New Haven, Conn.: Yale University Press, 1992), 292–93.

[5] Frank Lawrence Owsley Jr. and Gene A. Smith, *Filibusters and Expansionists: Jeffersonian Manifest Destiny, 1800–1821* (Tuscaloosa: University of Alabama Press, 1997), 141–63; Fred Anderson and Andrew Cayton, *The Dominion of War: Empire and Liberty in North America, 1500–2000* (New York: Viking, 2005), 166–238.

[6] John Opie, *The Law of the Land: Two Hundred Years of American Farmland Policy* (Lincoln: University of Nebraska Press, 1987), 40.

[7] Anderson and Cayton, *The Dominion of War*, 1–246; Arthur N. Gilbert, "The American Indian and United States Diplomatic History," *History Teacher* 8, no. 2 (February 1975): 229–41.

[8] Linda S. Hudson, *Mistress of Manifest Destiny: A Biography of Jane McManus Storm Cazneau, 1807–1878* (Austin: Texas State Historical Association, 2001), 58–62; Robert Sampson has questioned Hudson's attribution in *John L. O'Sullivan and His Times* (Kent, Ohio: Kent State University Press, 2003), 244–45.

[9] Sam W. Haynes, *Unfinished Revolution: The Early American Republic in a British World* (Charlottesville: University of Virginia Press, 2010), 177–229.

[10] Nineteenth-century Americans promoted the idea of a common "Anglo-Saxon" identity as a way to unify white Americans of different ethnic backgrounds. By the 1840s,

Americans whose ancestors hailed from Germany, Holland, Scandinavia, England, Scotland, and eventually Ireland identified themselves as Anglo-Saxons and defined themselves in opposition to those outside this fictional racial group.

[11] John Mack Faragher, *Women and Men on the Overland Trail*, rev. ed. (New Haven, Conn.: Yale University Press, 2001), 20–22.

[12] Rodrigo Lazo, *Writing to Cuba: Filibustering and Cuban Exiles in the United States* (Chapel Hill: University of North Carolina Press, 2005), 4–10.

[13] Brian DeLay, *War of a Thousand Deserts: Indian Raids and the U.S.-Mexican War* (New Haven, Conn.: Yale University Press, 2008), 35–85; Pekka Hämäläinen, *The Comanche Empire* (New Haven, Conn.: Yale University Press, 2008), 141–238.

[14] Daniel Walker Howe, *What Hath God Wrought: The Transformation of America, 1815–1848* (New York: Oxford University Press, 2007), 708–43.

[15] Amy S. Greenberg, "The Mexican-American War," in *The Princeton Encyclopedia of American Political History*, ed. Michael Kazin (Princeton, N.J.: Princeton University Press, 2010), 2:493–97.

[16] David Pletcher, *The Diplomacy of Annexation: Texas, Oregon, and the Mexican War* (Columbia: University of Missouri Press, 1973), 609–11; DeLay, *War of a Thousand Deserts*, 141–93.

[17] Richard Griswold Del Castillo, *The Treaty of Guadalupe Hidalgo: A Legacy of Conflict* (Norman: University of Oklahoma Press, 1992), 62–107.

[18] Willard Carl Klunder, *Lewis Cass and the Politics of Moderation* (Kent, Ohio: Kent State University Press, 1996), 165, 173.

[19] Peter H. Smith, *Talons of the Eagle: Dynamics of U.S.-Latin American Relations* (New York: Oxford University Press, 2000), 24.

[20] Ibid., 24–25.

[21] Albert Weinberg, *Manifest Destiny: A Study of Nationalist Expansionism in American History* (1935; repr., Chicago: Quadrangle Books, 1963), 201; Klunder, *Lewis Cass*, 289.

[22] Eric T. L. Love, *Race over Empire: Racism and U.S. Imperialism, 1865–1900* (Chapel Hill: University of North Carolina Press, 2004).

[23] Andrew C. Isenberg, *The Destruction of the Bison: An Environmental History, 1750–1920* (New York: Cambridge University Press, 2000).

[24] Social Darwinism was a popular late-nineteenth-century theory that a natural struggle between nations and the races would result in the "survival of the fittest." Strong people and races would rightfully thrive and dominate, while the weak would die.

[25] Paul Kramer, *The Blood of Government: Race, Empire, the United States, and the Philippines* (Chapel Hill: University of North Carolina Press, 2006), 87–158.

PART TWO

The Documents

1

Ideological Origins

1

WILLIAM BRADFORD

Of Plimoth Plantation
1650

William Bradford was a leader of the group of English Puritans, known as the Pilgrims, who left Holland to settle in North America in 1620. After a perilous journey aboard the Mayflower, *they landed in what is today Cape Cod, Massachusetts, and established Plymouth Colony. Bradford was elected governor in 1621 and reelected almost every year until his death in 1657. In 1630 Bradford began writing his two-volume account of the Pilgrims' flight from Europe and their establishment of a religious community in the New World; it was completed in 1650. In this excerpt, Bradford describes the Puritans' arrival in America in the winter of 1620 and links their survival to God's grace.*

Of Plimoth Plantation *was widely read in the centuries after its publication. In the nineteenth century, it was cited by proponents of Manifest Destiny as proof that from the beginning, the settlement of America was ordained by God. Bradford's representation of the Indians the Pilgrims encountered also offered a paradigm for Americans to follow in envisioning settlement as a race-based struggle between civilized Europeans and nonwhite savages.*

From William Bradford, *Bradford's History "Of Plimoth Plantation": From the Original Manuscript* (Boston: Wright and Potter, 1899), 94–97.

Being thus arived in a good harbor and brought safe to land, they fell upon their knees & blessed the God of heaven, who had brought them over the vast & furious ocean, and delivered them from all the periles & miseries therof, againe to set their feete on the firme and stable earth, their proper elemente. . . .

But hear I cannot but stay and make a pause, and stand half amased at this poore peoples presente condition; and so I thinke will the reader too, when he well considers the same. Being thus passed the vast ocean, and a sea of troubles before in their preparation (as may be remembred by that which wente before), they had now no freinds to wellcome them, nor inns to entertaine or refresh their weatherbeaten bodys, no houses or much less townes to repaire too, to seeke for succoure. It is recorded in scripture as a mercie to the apostle & his shipwraked company, that the barbarians shewed them no smale kindnes in refreshing them, but these savage barbarians, when they mette with them (as after will appeare) were readier to fill their sids full of arrows then otherwise. And for the season it was winter, and they that know the winters of that cuntrie know them to be sharp & violent, & subjecte to cruell & feirce stormes, deangerous to travill to known places, much more to serch an unknown coast. Besids, what could they see but a hidious & desolate wildernes, full of wild beasts & willd men? and what multituds ther might be of them they knew not. . . . What could now sustaine them but the spirite of God & his grace? May not & ought not the children of these fathers rightly say: *Our faithers were Englishmen which came over this great ocean, and were ready to perish in this willdernes; but they cried unto the Lord, and he heard their voyce, and looked on their adversitie, &c. Let them therfore praise the Lord, because he is good, & his mercies endure for ever. Yea, let them which have been redeemed of the Lord, shew how he hath delivered them from the hand of the oppressour. When they wandered in the deserte willdernes out of the way, and found no citie to dwell in, both hungrie, & thirstie, their sowle was overwhelmed in them. Let them confess before the Lord his loving kindnes, and his wonderfull works before the sons of men.*

JOHN WINTHROP

A Modell of Christian Charity

1630

In 1630 a second group of Puritans fleeing religious persecution in England made their way to the New World. They were determined to found a religious settlement of virtue and purity that would serve as a model for Puritans in England. As their ship neared land, John Winthrop, a college-educated lawyer and governor of the Massachusetts Bay Company, delivered a sermon to his fellow passengers. His address, "A Modell of Christian Charity," outlined his views of an ideal religious community and suggested how much was at stake in this experimental enterprise in the New World. On June 12, they landed in Salem, and the Commonwealth of Massachusetts was legally born.

The following excerpt from Winthrop's address identifies the Puritan mission as both divinely ordained and of singular, or exceptional, importance to the world. This exceptionalist view of American settlement provided an origin story for nineteenth-century proponents of Manifest Destiny. That America was established as a "citty upon a hill," and that the United States has created a model which other nations should follow, continues to inspire politicians to this day.

The Lord will be our God, and delight to dwell among us, as his oune people, and will command a blessing upon us in all our wayes. Soe that wee shall see much more of his wisdome, power, goodness and truthe, than formerly wee haue been acquainted with. Wee shall finde that the God of Israell is among us, when ten of us shall be able to resist a thousand of our enemies; when hee shall make us a prayse and glory that men shall say of succeeding plantations, "the Lord make it likely that of *New England.*" For wee must consider that wee shall be as a citty upon a hill. The eies of all people are uppon us. Soe that if wee shall deale falsely with our God in this worke wee haue undertaken, and soe cause him

From John Winthrop, "A Modell of Christian Charity," in *Collections of the Massachusetts Historical Society*, 3rd ser., ed. Charles C. Little and James Brown (Boston: Freeman and Bolles, 1838), 7:47.

to withdrawe his present help from us, wee shall be made a story and a by-word through the world. Wee shall open the mouthes of enemies to speake evill of the wayes of God, and all professors for God's sake. Wee shall shame the faces of many of God's worthy servants, and cause theire prayers to be turned into curses upon us till wee be consumed out of the good land whither wee are a goeing.

3

BENJAMIN FRANKLIN

Letter to Lord Kames
April 11, 1767

Colonial civil disobedience in the wake of the Stamp Act* led many in Britain to wonder about the rationality of American colonists. The Scottish philosopher Henry Home, Lord Kames, wrote inquiringly to his friend Benjamin Franklin on the matter. At the time, Franklin was the leading spokesman for American interests living in London. In his response of April 11, 1767, Franklin not only explained the sources of the conflict over the Stamp Act but also offered his views on the future of the American colonies. Well before the Revolution, Franklin articulated a vision of America's possible independence and greatness grounded in its potential territorial growth. Unfortunately, Kames never received Franklin's response: British authorities intercepted and confiscated this letter.

Upon the whole, I have lived so great a part of my life in Britain, and have formed so many friendships in it, that I love it, and sincerely wish it prosperity; and therefore wish to see that union, on which alone I think it can be secured and established. As to America, the advantages of such

---

***Stamp Act:** A direct tax imposed by Britain on the American colonies in 1765. Colonists were not represented in British Parliament, and objected to paying a tax they had not consented to.

From Benjamin Franklin to Lord Kames, April 11, 1767, in *The Works of Dr. Benjamin Franklin in Philosophy, Politics, and Morals . . .* , ed. William Temple Franklin (Philadelphia: William Duane, 1817), 6:62–63.

an union to her are not so apparent. She may suffer at present under the arbitrary power of this country; she may suffer for a while in a separation from it; but these are temporary evils which she will out-grow. Scotland and Ireland, are differently circumstanced. Confined by the sea, they can scarcely increase in numbers, wealth and strength, so as to overbalance England. But America, an immense territory, favoured by nature, with all advantages of climate, soils, great navigable rivers, lakes, &c. must become a great country, populous and mighty; and will, in a less time than is generally conceived, be able to shake off any shackles that may be imposed upon her, and perhaps place them on the imposers. In the mean time every act of oppression will sour their tempers, lessen greatly if not annihilate the profits of your commerce with them, and hasten their final revolt; for the seeds of liberty are universally found there, and nothing can eradicate them. And yet there remains among that people, so much respect, veneration, and affection for Britain, that if cultivated prudently, with a kind usage and tenderness for their privileges, they might be easily governed still for ages, without force or any considerable expense. But I do not see here a sufficient quantity of the wisdom that is necessary to produce such a conduct, and I lament the want of it.

2

Expansion in the Early Republic

4

RICHARD BUTLER

A Commissioner's View of the Ohio River Valley

1785

One of the biggest tasks facing Congress under America's first constitution, the Articles of Confederation, was the distribution of trans-Appalachian land ceded by Britain in the Treaty of Paris (1783). Congress hoped to sell the land northwest of the Ohio River and east of the Mississippi to finance America's war debt, but Indian people held sway over much of the region. In 1785 Congress directed General Richard Butler, a Revolutionary War veteran with experience fighting Indians, along with two other commissioners, to make a treaty with the powerful Shawnee tribe to facilitate congressional land distribution.

Butler, in the company of U.S. troops, traveled from his home in Pennsylvania along the Ohio River that fall. Although Congress had explicitly forbidden white settlement in the region prior to the federal sales, Butler and his companions encountered many squatters north of the Ohio. The commissioner warned them that they were violating the law and that U.S. soldiers would come and "destroy every house and improvement on the north side of the river." Some of the squatters were apologetic, but others made it clear that they viewed the immediate white settlement of the region as their natural right.

From "Journal of General Butler," ed. Neville B. Craig, *Olden Time* 2, no. 10 (October 1847): 440, 445–46.

The appeal of the fertile land along the Ohio was obvious to Butler. In the following passages from his diary, written in October 1785, Butler expresses a view of the region's future, clearly shaped by a belief in American exceptionalism. But his suggestion that future residents might form their own nation indicates how few people in the 1780s envisioned a continental destiny for the United States. Even avid American expansionists imagined multiple nations (modeled on the United States) occupying the vast land mass of North America. Butler decided to buy land for himself and on the same day warned squatters (with a proclamation) that their "improvements" would be destroyed by U.S. troops.

In January 1786, Butler and the other commissioners met with members of the "Shawanese" at Fort Finney, near present-day Cincinnati. Tribal representatives begrudgingly signed a treaty ceding a portion of the territory east of the Miami River to the United States. This treaty was quickly renounced by a majority of the Shawnees, who were perhaps not as much "disposed to peace" as Butler.

Butler's mission proved futile in ending armed conflict between whites and Indians in the region. Within a year, the Kentucky militia burned a Shawnee town to the ground. Just a few years later, the Shawnees took the lead in forming a confederation of tribes in the Old Northwest committed to resisting U.S. expansion. In 1791, Butler was one of more than 600 American soldiers killed by the confederacy of Northwest Indians at the Battle of the Wabash, the single greatest victory of Indian people over the United States Army.

The lands on each side [of the Ohio] are really delightful. On one side of every bend is a grand and extensive bottom of very rich land; and opposite high and beautiful hills of good land, generally on easy slope or ascent, and seldom rocky; and will, in my opinion, before many years be the seats of opulent farmers: and if properly governed will add strength and riches to the confederacy. But I think the more easily the first settlers are led in to government, and convinced of their dependence on the old States, the less probability of their attempting to break off. . . . One thing will endear them to the old States, which is, protection from the Indians, this can be done very easy, once we have possession of the frontier posts, and which will be difficult till that takes place. . . .

The lands here are really beautiful, and very rich; the majestic Ohio rolling gently along within the most delightful banks that ever enclosed a river; and in a few years must be the happy abode of thousands who, with moderate industry may obtain the greatest profusion of the necessaries of life; the soil being so abundantly rich and fertile, and the climate inferior to none on the globe. . . .

. . . Here may the industrious and broken hearted farmer, tired with the slavery of the unfortunate situation in which he was born, lay down his burthen and find rest on these peaceful and plenteous plains; here may Iberia,[1] Britain and Scotia,[2] pour out their superabundant sons and daughters, who with cheerful hearts, and industrious hands, will wipe away the tear of tyrannic toil, and join the children of America in the easy labors of comfort and plenty, and bless the providence of that power who hath directed them to such a land; yes, they will be good, respectful, and grateful citizens, the greatest enemies of kingly power, and will support with you, ye heroic sons of Independence, and your children's children, those honors, those blessings earned by your toils, blood, and treasure; and sing the praises of God in temples yet to form, who led you to the battles, and conquest of the unwise and tyrannic George the third. They will also in the anniversary song transmit your virtues and heroism to the children of future time, whose hearts shall beat high in emulating their progenitors, and keeping sacred the scroll of Independence. . . .

Here I found young Col. Lewis,[3] who is a most sensible young gentleman, very interesting and communicative. I find by him that the Shawanese are very much disposed to peace. . . . We dined on the point, treated Col. Lewis with attention, who received it very politely. I inquired if they did not intend to lay out, a town at the point, he told me it was laid out and the lots generally sold; but if I wanted a lot, or more, I might still be supplied, as many of the lots were forfeited. I told him I would purchase, on which we went to look over the ground, and he took me up the Ohio bank to a fine dry lot which fronts the street on the river Ohio, a street that runs at right angles from the river and the main street, or first parallel street with the Ohio, which gives it three fronts, being west, north and east. This I agreed for, and am to pay him ten pounds for it. We then went to the banks of the Kanhawa[4] and examined it. I expressed a wish to have a lot on it, he told me the family had reserved several front lots for themselves, and he imagined he could procure me No. 3 from the point, which is a delightful situation, has on it a fine plumb tree, some

---

[1] The Iberian Peninsula: Spain and Portugal.
[2] Scotland.
[3] Andrew Lewis.
[4] A tributary of the Ohio River.

peach trees, &c., planted by one Dr. Smith. . . . I also told him I would pay him now if he chose it, as I had the cash ready and would rather pay it at once. He said he would not take the money till he had the draft completed, which he expects will be this fall. . . .

This day we passed several improvements on the north side. Had a proclamation put up at one of the houses above Kanhawa. This delightful country involuntarily draws from my pen praises; it is fine, it is rich, and only wants the cultivating hand of man to render it the joyous seat of happy thousands. Here are the wild animals provided for the assistance of the first settlers. Here are the finest and most excellent sites for farms, cities, and towns. This seems provided as a reward for the adventurous and industrious, by the Divine hand, whose good providence appear in all his works. Here we have nothing to do but spring from our boats among flocks of turkeys, kill as we please for sport or gust; the bear growls in your hearing, and the deer, timid by nature, bounds along before your eye; in short, there is no end to the beauty and plenty.

5

COUNCIL OF 1793

To the Commissioners of the United States
August 16, 1793

The contested ownership of land west of the Appalachian Mountains proved a continuing source of friction in the early Republic. The fact that the British had forbidden settlement in the region had led many westerners to support independence in 1776. Federal attempts to open the region to settlement in the 1780s and early 1790s had been thwarted by an increasingly unified confederation of tribes who occupied the region now known as the Old Northwest. They renounced treaties that they believed to be illegitimate (see Document 4) and refused to negotiate over the future status of their land east of the Mississippi. After insisting that the Ohio

From "To the Commissioners of the United States, August 16, 1793," in *American State Papers, Senate, 3rd Congress, 1st Session, Indian Affairs* (Washington, D.C.: Government Printing Office, 1832), 1:356–57.

*River remain the boundary between U.S. and Indian land, the confedera-
tion defeated the U.S. Army in battles in 1790 and 1791.*

*Congress dispatched yet another group of commissioners to resolve the
impasse. They met with Indian representatives in 1793 and argued that
because white settlement in the region was an established fact, it was
impossible for the federal government to uphold the Ohio River boundary. A decade earlier, the federal government had directed U.S. troops
to destroy squatters' homes and other structures. But the commissioners
now pointed to the existing crops and homes of settlers as justification for
U.S. ownership of Indian land. According to both enlightenment philosophy and American public opinion, such improvements gave the settlers
a stronger claim to the land than that of the tribes who had left it fallow.
The time had come, the commissioners said, for the Indians to sign over
that land to the United States.*

*Sixteen tribes met in council and responded to the commissioners with
the following letter, which was delivered by two Wyandot (Huron) Indians
on August 16, 1793. In the excerpt that follows, they offer their own solution to the problem of white settlement in the region. Notice how the tribes
engage with the European idea of "improvement" to make their case.*

*The commissioners immediately replied by letter that since it was "im-
possible to make the river Ohio the boundary between your lands and the
lands of the United States. . . . The negotiation is therefore at an end."
The conclusion of the commissioners' letter appears to have been intended
more for American readers than for the tribes: "Knowing the upright and
liberal views of the United States . . . we trust that impartial judges will
not attribute the continence of the war to them."*

*This decades-long conflict between white settlers and Indian people in
the Old Northwest was ultimately resolved at the Battle of Fallen Timbers
in 1794 and the subsequent Treaty of Greenville in 1795, which turned
much of the region over to the United States.*

BROTHERS: We have received your speech, dated the 31st of last month,
and it has been interpreted to all the different nations: we have been
long in sending you an answer, because of the great importance of the
subject. But we now answer it fully, having given it all the consideration
in our power. . . .

BROTHERS: Money, to us, is of no value, and to most of us unknown:
and as no consideration whatever can induce us to sell the lands on

which we get sustenance for our women and children, we hope we may be allowed to point out a mode by which your settlers may be easily removed, and peace thereby obtained.

BROTHERS: We know that these settlers are poor, or they would never have ventured to live in a country which has been in continual trouble ever since they crossed the Ohio. Divide, therefore, this large sum of money, which you have offered to us, among these people: give to each, also, a proportion of what you say you would give to us, annually, over and above this very large sum of money: and, we are persuaded, they would most readily accept of it, in lieu of the lands you sold them. If you add, also, the great sums you must expend in raising and paying armies, with a view to force us to yield you our country, you will certainly have more than sufficient for the purposes of re-paying these settlers for all their labor and their improvements.

BROTHERS: You have talked to us about concessions. It appears strange that you should expect any from us, who have only been defending our just rights against your invasions. We want peace. Restore to us our country, and we shall be enemies no longer.

BROTHERS: You make one concession to us by offering us your money; and another by having agreed to do us justice, after having long, and injuriously, withheld it—we mean in the acknowledgment you have now made, that the King of England never did, nor ever had a right to give you our country, by the treaty of peace. And you want to make this act of common justice a great part of your concessions: and seem to expect that, because you have at last acknowledged our independence, we should, for such a favor, surrender to you our country. . . .

We desire you to consider, brothers, that our only demand is the peaceable possession of a small part of our once great country. Look back, and review the lands from whence we have been driven to this spot. We can retreat no farther, because the country behind hardly affords food for its present inhabitants; and we have therefore resolved to leave our bones in this small space to which we are now confined.

BROTHERS: We shall be persuaded that you mean to do us justice, if you agree that the Ohio shall remain the boundary line between us. If you will not consent thereto, our meeting will be altogether unnecessary. This is the great point which we hoped would have been explained before you left your homes, as our message last fall was principally directed to obtain that information.

Done in general council, at the foot of the Miami Rapids, the 13th day of August, 1793.

NATIONS.

WYANDOTS,	PATTAWATAMIES,
SEVEN NATIONS OF CANADA,	CONNOYS,
DELAWARES,	MUNSEES,
SHAWANESE,	NANTEKOKIES,
MIAMIES,	MOHICANS,
OTTAWAS,	MESSASAGOES,
CHIPPEWAS,	CREEKS,
SENECAS OF THE GLAIZE,	CHEROKEES.

6

JEDIDIAH MORSE

The American Geography

1792

Jedidiah Morse was a Massachusetts minister, geographer, educator, and firm nationalist. He was also one of the first to recognize that to promote a love of country among children, the United States needed schoolbooks written by Americans. Morse, "the Father of American Geography," set preaching aside to write schoolbooks. He published his first American geography in 1784. A much-expanded volume, The American Geography, *followed in 1789, to great acclaim and frequent reprinting. Until his death in 1826, Morse revised* The American Geography *every few years to keep up with current events and changes in U.S. settlement. In 1820 Morse served as an agent of the U.S. War Department investigating the plight of Indian peoples.*

Morse's geographies were openly celebratory about the march west. As early as the 1780s, Morse confidently predicted the growth of an American empire in North America. The following passage from the 1792 second edition of The American Geography *considers the fate of Americans in the territory owned by Spain west of the Mississippi. Note how pride in the excellence of American "government, religion, and educa-*

From Jedidiah Morse, *The American Geography; or, A View of the Present Situation of the United States of America*, 2nd ed. (London: John Stockdale, 1792), 468–69.

tion" leads him to a remarkably ambitious conclusion about the growth of the nation.

It has been supposed by some, that all settlers who go beyond the Missisippi [*sic*], will be forever lost to the United States. There is, I believe, little danger of this, provided they are not provoked to withdraw their friendship. The emigrants will be made up of citizens of the United States. They will carry along with them their manners and customs, their habits of government, religion, and education; and as they are to be indulged with religious freedom, and with the privilege of making their own laws, and of conducting education upon their own plans; these *American* habits will undoubtedly be cherished. If so, they will be Americans in fact, though nominally the subjects of Spain.

It is true Spain will draw a revenue from them, but in return they will enjoy peculiar commercial advantages, the benefit of which will be experienced by the United States, and perhaps be an ample compensation for the loss of so many citizens as may migrate thither. In short, this settlement, if conducted with judgment and prudence, may be mutually serviceable both to Spain and the United States. It may prevent jealousies—lessen national prejudices—promote religious toleration, preserve harmony, and be a medium of trade reciprocally advantageous.

Besides, it is well known that empire has been travelling from east to west. Probably her last and broadest feat will be America. Here the sciences, and the arts of civilized life, are to receive their highest improvement. Here civil and religious liberty are to flourish, unchecked by the cruel hand of civil or ecclesiastical tyranny. Here genius, aided by all the improvements of former ages, is to be exerted in humanizing mankind—in expanding and enriching their minds with religious and philosophical knowledge, and in planning and executing a form of government, which shall involve all the excellencies of former governments, with as few of their defects as is consistent with the imperfection of human affairs, and which shall be calculated to protect and unite, in a manner consistent with the natural rights of mankind, the largest empire that ever existed. Elevated with these prospects, which are not merely the visions of fancy, we cannot but anticipate the period, as not far distant, when the AMERICAN EMPIRE will comprehend millions of souls, west of the Missisippi. Judging upon probable grounds, the Missisippi was never designed as the western boundary of the American empire. The God of nature never intended that some of the best part of his earth should be inhabited by the subjects of a monarch 4000 miles from them. And may we not venture to predict, that, when the rights of mankind shall be more fully known, and the knowledge of them is fast increasing both in Europe and America, the power of European potentates will be confined to Europe, and their present American dominions, become like the United States, free, sovereign, and independent empires.

7

FISHER AMES

Letter to Thomas Dwight

October 31, 1803

Federalists, particularly in New England, generally opposed the annexation of additional territory to the young United States. They angrily denounced Democratic-Republican schemes to annex Florida and portions of Canada. Many also contested Jefferson's Louisiana Purchase, despite the fact that it brought the valuable shipping port of New Orleans under U.S. control and greatly reduced the French threat.

In part this can be blamed on partisanship: Any victory for Jefferson's Democratic-Republicans was a loss for the opposition. But Federalists also worried that expansion to the west would bring the United States in conflict with England and Spain, that it would undermine the balance of power between the states, and that democratic practices would be impossible to maintain over an extended territory.

Fisher Ames, a former U.S. representative from Massachusetts, was not the only Federalist aghast at the idea of adding the mixed-race and largely Catholic population of Louisiana to the Republic. Ames composed the letter excerpted here after reading a copy of the Louisiana Purchase Treaty (which he sarcastically deems "delightful") sent to him by Representative Thomas Dwight.

Fisher Ames to Thomas Dwight, October 31, 1803. From Fisher Ames, *Works of Fisher Ames* (Boston: T. B. Wait, 1809), 484.

DEDHAM, October 31st, 1803.

My dear Friend:

I have this morning received by post your delightful treaty, and S. H. Smith's paper,[1] and your esteemed favour,[2] in which you give me a particular account of yourself and your accommodations. This latter is really more interesting to my curiosity and feelings than the rest of the contents under cover. . . .

Having bought an empire, who is to be emperour? The sovereign people—and what people? all, or only the people of the dominant states, and the dominant demagogues in those states, who call themselves the people? As in old Rome, Marius or Sylla, or Cesar, Pompey, Antony, or Lepidus will vote themselves provinces and triumphs.

I have as loyal and respectful an opinion as possible of the *sincerity in folly* of our rulers. But, surely, it exceeds all my credulity and candour on that head, to suppose even they can contemplate a republican form as practicable, honest, or free, if applied when it is so manifestly inapplicable to the government of one third of God's earth. It could not, I think, even maintain forms; and as to principles, the otters would as soon obey and give them effect as the *Gallo-Hispano-Indian omnium gatherum* of savages and adventurers, whose pure morals are expected to sustain and glorify our republick.

[1] A newspaper.
[2] Personal letter.

8

THOMAS JEFFERSON

Second Inaugural Address

March 4, 1805

Perhaps the greatest accomplishment of Thomas Jefferson's presidency was the purchase of the vast territory of Louisiana from France in 1803 for $15 million. But the purchase was also of questionable legality; the Constitution did not specify the right of a president to purchase land. As

From Thomas Jefferson, "Second Inaugural Address, March 4, 1805," in *Presidents' Messages: Inaugural, Annual and Special from 1789 to 1846*, ed. Edwin Williams (New York: Edward Walker, 1846), 1:174–75.

Fisher Ames made clear (see Document 7), not all Americans supported territorial expansion in the early nineteenth century. And much of the territory was under the firm control of Indian peoples. Perhaps it is not surprising that although the Louisiana Purchase was one of the signature events of western expansionism, the president waited until midway through his second inaugural address to discuss it. In the portion of the address reprinted here, Jefferson responds to critics by articulating his belief in American exceptionalism and destiny. Like Ames, Jefferson places the purchase in a racial context, but his view of the future of the "aboriginal inhabitants of these countries" led him to a very different conclusion about the costs and benefits of western settlement.

I know that the acquisition of Louisiana has been disapproved by some, from a candid apprehension that the enlargement of our territory would endanger its union. But who can limit the extent to which the federative principle may operate effectively? The larger our association, the less will it be shaken by local passions; and in any view, is it not better that the opposite bank of the Mississippi should be settled by our own brethren and children, than by strangers of another family? With which shall we be most likely to live in harmony and friendly intercourse? . . .

The aboriginal inhabitants of these countries I have regarded with the commiseration their history inspires. Endowed with the faculties and the rights of men, breathing an ardent love of liberty and independence, and occupying a country which left them no desire but to be undisturbed, the stream of overflowing population from other regions directed itself on these shores; without power to divert, or habits to contend against, they have been overwhelmed by the current, or driven before it; now reduced within limits too narrow for the hunter's state, humanity enjoins us to teach them agriculture and the domestic arts; to encourage them to that industry which alone can enable them to maintain their place in existence, and to prepare them in time for that state of society, which to bodily comforts adds the improvement of the mind and morals. We have therefore liberally furnished them with the implements of husbandry and household use; we have placed among them instructors in the arts of first necessity; and they are covered with the ægis of the law against aggressors from among ourselves.

But the endeavors to enlighten them on the fate which awaits their present course of life, to induce them to exercise their reason, follow its dictates, and change their pursuits with the change of circumstances,

have powerful obstacles to encounter; they are combated by the habits
of their bodies, prejudice of their minds, ignorance, pride, and the influence of interested and crafty individuals among them, who feel themselves something in the present order of things, and fear to become
nothing in any other. These persons inculcate a sanctimonious rever-
ence for the customs of their ancestors; that whatsoever they did, must
be done through all time; that reason is a false guide, and to advance
under its counsel, in their physical, moral, or political condition, is
perilous innovation; that their duty is to remain as their Creator made
them, ignorance being safety, and knowledge full of danger; in short,
my friends, among them is seen the action and counteraction of good
sense and bigotry; they too have their anti-philosophers, who find an
interest in keeping things in their present state, who dread reformation,
and exert all their faculties to maintain the ascendency of habit over the
duty of improving our reason and obeying its mandates.

9

TECUMSEH

Appeal to the Osages

1811

*The Shawnee diplomat and warrior Tecumseh, who saw his homeland in
northern Indiana Territory invaded by white settlers, believed that only a
pan-Indian confederacy could defeat the encroaching United States. In his
efforts to unite Indian peoples, Tecumseh traveled from village to village
in what is now the Southeast and Midwest from August 1811 to January
1812. On that journey, he met with Creeks, Chickasaws, Choctaws, Osages,
western Shawnees and Delawares, and perhaps a dozen other tribes. A
skilled orator, he allegedly delivered this speech to a band of Osages in
1811, although the authenticity of this account has been questioned. The
original transcription, excerpted here, appeared in a narrative by a white
critic of U.S. Indian policy, John Dunn Hunter, who claimed to have heard*

From John Dunn Hunter, *The American Book of Indians, Containing the Most Interesting
Narratives of Indian Chiefs and Indian Wars Now Extant* (Dayton, Ohio: Moore, Clark,
1854), 49–52.

*Tecumseh deliver the speech. That Tecumseh met with the Osages in 1811
is beyond doubt. What is less certain is that Tecumseh used these words
to address the Osages, particularly given that Tecumseh's account of white
duplicity and greed closely aligns with that of his translator.*

*Tecumseh's efforts to unify Indian peoples met with limited success. He
and his confederacy fought on the side of the British in the War of 1812;
he was killed by American forces in 1813.*

"*Brothers*—We all belong to one family, we are all children of the Great
Spirit; we walk in the same path; slake our thirst at the same spring; and
now affairs of the greatest concern, lead us to smoke the pipe around
the same council fire!

Brothers—We are friends; we must assist each other to bear our bur-
dens. The blood of many of our fathers and brothers has run like water
on the ground, to satisfy the avarice of the white men. We, ourselves, are
threatened with a great evil; nothing will pacify them but the destruction
of all the red men.

Brothers—When the white men first set foot on our grounds, they
were hungry; they had no place on which to spread their blankets, or to
kindle their fires. They were feeble, they could do nothing for themselves.
Our fathers commiserated their distress, and sheared with them whatever the Great Spirit had given his red children. They gave them food
when hungry, medicine when sick, spread skins for them to sleep on,
and gave them grounds, that they might hunt and raise corn. Brothers,
the white people are like poisonous serpents; when chilled, they are
feeble and harmless, but invigorate them with warmth, and they sting
their benefactors to death.

The white people came among us feeble: and now we have made
them strong, they wish to kill us, or drive us back, as they would wolves
and panthers.

Brothers—The white men are not friends to the Indians; at first they
only asked for land sufficient for a wigwam, now, nothing will satisfy them
but the whole of our hunting grounds, from the rising to the setting sun.

Brothers—The white men want more than our hunting grounds—
they wish to kill our warriors; they would even kill our old men, women,
and little ones.

Brothers—Many winters ago, there was no land—the sun did not
rise and set: all was darkness. The Great Spirit made all things. He gave
the white people a home beyond the great waters. He supplied these
grounds with game, and gave them to his red children, and he gave
them strength and courage to defend them.

Brothers—My people wish for peace, the red men all wish for peace: but where the white people are, there is no peace for them, except it be in the bosom of our mother.

Brothers—The white men despise and cheat the Indians; they abuse and insult them; they do not think the red men sufficiently good to live.

The red men have borne many and great injuries; they ought to suffer them no longer. My people will not; they are determined on vengeance; they have taken up the tomakawk; they will make it fat with blood—they will drink the blood of the white people.

Brothers—My people are brave and numerous, but the white people are too strong for them alone. I wish you to take up the tomahawk with them. If we all unite, we will cause the rivers to stain the great waters with their blood.

Brothers—If you do not unite with us, they will first destroy us, and then you will fall an easy prey to them. They have destroyed many nations of red men, because they were not united, because they were not friends to each other.

Brothers—The white people send runners amongst us; they wish to make us enemies, that they may sweep over, and desolate our hunting grounds, like devastating winds, or rushing waters.

Brothers—Our Great Father, over the great waters, is angry with the white people, our enemies. He will send his brave warriors against them; he will send us rifles, and whatever else we want—he is our friend, and we are his children.

Brothers—Who are the white people that we should fear them? They cannot run fast, and are good marks to shoot at; they are only men; our fathers have killed many of them; we are not squaws, and we will stain the earth red with their blood.

Brothers—The Great Spirit is angry with our enemies—he speaks in thunder, and the earth swallows up villages, and drinks up the Mississippi.[1] The great waters will cover their low-lands, their corn cannot grow, and the Great Spirit will sweep those who escape to the hills, from the earth with his terrible breath.

Brothers—We must be united; we must smoke the same pipe; we must fight each other's battles; an[d] more than all, we must love the Great Spirit; he is for us; he will destroy our enemies, and make all his red children happy."

---

[1] A series of earthquakes in 1811–1812 centered on New Madrid, Missouri Territory, was taken as a serious omen by Indian peoples in the region and may have helped Tecumseh's cause.

3

Pushing West

10

ANDREW JACKSON

State of the Union Address
December 6, 1830

When the famous Indian fighter Andrew Jackson won election in 1828, he became the first president who lived west of the Appalachian Mountains. In his first annual message to Congress in 1829, he fulfilled a campaign promise when he called on Congress to enact legislation to remove the "Five Civilized Tribes" of the Southeast—the Cherokees, Creeks, Choctaws, Chickasaws, and Seminoles—to west of the Mississippi River. After bitter congressional debate, Congress passed the Indian Removal Act, and Jackson signed it into law on May 28, 1830.

At the time of Jackson's second State of the Union address, the Choctaws and Chickasaws had agreed to removal; the Creeks, Cherokees, and Seminoles had not. Opposition to the policy was rife not only among Indian peoples but also among whites in the Northeast and members of the opposition Whig party generally. In this address, Jackson attempted to make removal sound beneficial to all, but in truth his racist view of even the settled and Christianized tribes of the Southeast as "savages" led him to equate progress strictly with the advancement of American expansion. Note the language Jackson uses to describe Indians in this excerpt and how he disingenuously equates the forced migration of Indian removal with the enthusiastic and voluntary western migration of white settlers.

From Andrew Jackson, "Second Annual Message, December 6, 1830," in *A Compilation of the Messages and Papers of the Presidents, 1789–1897*, comp. James D. Richardson (New York: Bureau of National Literature, 1898), 2:519–23.

By employing the military in the service of expansion, Jackson set an important precedent in the drive to fulfill the nation's Manifest Destiny.

It gives me pleasure to announce to Congress that the benevolent policy of the Government, steadily pursued for nearly thirty years, in relation to the removal of the Indians beyond the white settlements is approaching to a happy consummation. . . .

The consequences of a speedy removal will be important to the United States, to individual States, and to the Indians themselves. The pecuniary advantages which it promises to the Government are the least of its recommendations. It puts an end to all possible danger of collision between the authorities of the General and State Governments on account of the Indians. It will place a dense and civilized population in large tracts of country now occupied by a few savage hunters. By opening the whole territory between Tennessee on the north and Louisiana on the south to the settlement of the whites it will incalculably strengthen the southwestern frontier and render the adjacent States strong enough to repel future invasions without remote aid. It will relieve the whole State of Mississippi and the western part of Alabama of Indian occupancy, and enable those States to advance rapidly in population, wealth, and power. It will separate the Indians from immediate contact with settlements of whites; free them from the power of the States; enable them to pursue happiness in their own way and under their own rude institutions; will retard the progress of decay, which is lessening their numbers, and perhaps cause them gradually, under the protection of the Government and through the influence of good counsels, to cast off their savage habits and become an interesting, civilized, and Christian community. These consequences, some of them so certain and the rest so probable, make the complete execution of the plan sanctioned by Congress at their last session an object of much solicitude.

Toward the aborigines of the country no one can indulge a more friendly feeling than myself, or would go further in attempting to reclaim them from their wandering habits and make them a happy, prosperous people. . . .

Humanity has often wept over the fate of the aborigines of this country, and Philanthropy has been long busily employed in devising means to avert it, but its progress has never for a moment been arrested, and one by one have many powerful tribes disappeared from the earth. To follow to the tomb the last of his race and to tread on the graves of extinct nations excite melancholy reflections. But true philanthropy reconciles the mind to these vicissitudes as it does to the extinction of one generation to make room for another. In the monuments and fortresses of an unknown people, spread over the extensive regions of the West, we behold the memorials of a once powerful race, which was exterminated or has disappeared to make room for the existing savage tribes. Nor is there anything in this which, upon a comprehensive view of the general interests of the human race, is to be regretted. Philanthropy could not wish to see this continent restored to the condition in which it was found by our forefathers. What good man would prefer a country covered with forests and ranged by a few thousand savages to our extensive Republic, studded with cities, towns, and prosperous farms, embellished with all the improvements which art can devise or industry execute, occupied by more than 12,000,000 happy people, and filled with all the blessings of liberty, civilization, and religion?

The present policy of the Government is but a continuation of the same progressive change by a milder process. The tribes which occupied the countries now constituting the Eastern States were annihilated or have melted away to make room for the whites. The waves of population and civilization are rolling to the westward, and we now propose to acquire the countries occupied by the red men of the South and West by a fair exchange, and, at the expense of the United States, to send them to a land where their existence may be prolonged and perhaps made perpetual. Doubtless it will be painful to leave the graves of their fathers; but what do they more than our ancestors did or than our children are now doing? To better their condition in an unknown land our forefathers left all that was dear in earthly objects. Our children by thousands yearly leave the land of their birth to seek new homes in distant regions. Does Humanity weep at these painful separations from everything, animate and inanimate, with which the young heart has become entwined? Far from it. It is rather a source of joy that our country affords scope where our young population may range unconstrained in body or in mind, developing the power and faculties of man in their highest perfection. These remove hundreds and almost thousands of miles at their own expense, purchase the lands they occupy, and support themselves at their new homes from the moment of their arrival. Can it be cruel in this Government when, by events which it can not control, the Indian is made discontented in his ancient home to purchase his lands, to give him a new and extensive territory, to pay the expense of his removal, and support him a year in his new abode? How many thousands of our own people would gladly embrace the opportunity of removing to the West on such conditions! If the offers made to the Indians were extended to them, they would be hailed with gratitude and joy.

And is it supposed that the wandering savage has a stronger attachment to his home than the settled, civilized Christian? Is it more afflicting to him to leave the graves of his fathers than it is to our brothers and children? Rightly considered, the policy of the General Government toward the red man is not only liberal, but generous. He is unwilling to submit to the laws of the States and mingle with their population. To save him from this alternative, or perhaps utter annihilation, the General Government kindly offers him a new home, and proposes to pay the whole expense of his removal and settlement. . . .

May we not hope, therefore, that all good citizens, and none more zealously than those who think the Indians oppressed by subjection to the laws of the States, will unite in attempting to open the eyes of those children of the forest to their true condition, and by a speedy removal to relieve them from all the evils, real or imaginary, present or prospective, with which they may be supposed to be threatened.

11

BLACK HAWK

Encroachment by White Settlers

1832

Not all of the victims of Indian removal resided in what is now the Southeast. In 1832 Sac and Fox Indians attempted to reclaim ancestral land in northwestern Illinois, despite having ceded that land to the United States in earlier treaties, which they considered invalid. The result was a brief but bloody conflict between the tribes and the Illinois militia called the Black Hawk War, the defeat of the tribes, and their banishment west of the Mississippi. The sixty-seven-year-old Sac war chief Ma-ka-tai-me-she-kia-kiak, also known as Black Hawk, was captured, held in military barracks, and then taken on a tour of the eastern United States, where he met with President Andrew Jackson and assorted other luminaries.

From Black Hawk, *Life of Ma-ka-tai-me-she-kia-kiak or Black Hawk* (Boston: Russell, Odiorne and Metcalf, 1834), 48, 86–87, 102–7, 109.

His dignified behavior inspired sympathy among residents of the North-east, most of whom had never seen a Native American. As a result, many ordinary Americans, including women, became critics of Indian removal.

Black Hawk dictated his life story to a government interpreter in 1832, soon after his return from U.S. custody. Unfortunately, no original tran-script of the account exists, but according to the interpreter, Black Hawk's goal was to justify his actions in the war. The resulting document, Life of Ma-ka-tai-me-she-kia-kiak or Black Hawk, *became the first published Native American autobiography when it appeared in print in Cincin-nati in 1833. In the following excerpt, Black Hawk describes the conflicts between white settlers and Indians after he unknowingly signed a treaty handing his village over to the United States in 1816. This document indicates both how different understandings of landownership between Indians and whites had tragic results and how individual plots of land became the ground for both negotiation and conflict in western expansion.*

Why did the Great Spirit ever send the whites to this island, to drive us from our homes, and introduce among us *poisonous liquors, disease and death*? They should have remained on the island where the Great Spirit first placed them. But I will proceed with my story. My memory, how-ever, is not very good, since my late visit to the white people. I have still a buzzing in my ears, from the noise—and may give some parts of my story out of place; but I will endeavor to be correct....

... [In 1816] for the first time, I touched the goose quill to the treaty—not knowing, however, that, by that act, I consented to give away my village. Had that been explained to me, I should have opposed it, and never would have signed their treaty, as my recent conduct will clearly prove.

What do we know of the manner of the laws and customs of the white people? They might buy our bodies for dissection, and we would touch the goose quill to confirm it, without knowing what we are doing. This was the case with myself and people in touching the goose quill the first time.

We can only judge of what is proper and right by our standard of right and wrong, which differs widely from the whites, if I have been cor-rectly informed. The whites *may do bad* all their lives, and then, if they are *sorry for it* when about to die, *all is well*! But with us it is different: we must continue throughout our lives to do what we conceive to be good. If we have corn and meat, and know of a family that have none, we divide with them. If we have more blankets than sufficient, and others have not enough, we must give to them that want. . . .

I . . . hunted that winter on the Two-Rivers.[1] The whites were now settling the country fast. I was out one day hunting in a bottom,[2] and met three white men. They accused me of killing their hogs. I denied it; but they would not listen to me. One of them took my gun out of my hand and fired it off—then took out the flint, gave back my gun, and commenced beating me with sticks, and ordered me off. I was so much bruised that I could not sleep for several nights.

Some time after this occurrence, one of my camp cut a bee-tree, and carried the honey to his lodge. A party of white men soon followed, and told him the bee-tree was theirs, and that he had no right to cut it. He pointed to the honey and told them to take it; they were not satisfied with this, but took all the packs of skins that he had collected during the winter, to pay his trader and clothe his family with in the spring, and carried them off!

How could we like such people, who treated us so unjustly? . . .

This summer[3] our agent came to live at Rock Island. He treated us well, and gave us good advice. I visited him and the trader[4] very often during the summer, and, for the first time, heard talk of our having to leave my village. The trader, explained to me the terms of the treaty that had been made, and said we would be obliged to leave the Illinois side of the Mississippi, and advised us to select a good place for our village, and remove to it in the spring. He pointed out the difficulties we would have to encounter if we remained at our village on Rock river. . . .

The party [of Indians] opposed to removing called upon me for my opinion. I gave it freely. . . . I was of opinion that the white people had plenty of land, and would never take our village from us. . . . We started to our hunting grounds, in good hopes that something would be done for us. During the winter I received information that three families of whites had arrived at our village and destroyed some of our lodges, and were making fences and dividing our corn-fields for their own use—*and were quarreling among themselves about their lines in the division!* I immediately started for Rock river[,] a distance of ten days' travel, and on my arrival found the report to be true. I went to my lodge, and saw a family occupying it. I wished to talk with them but they could not understand me. I then went to Rock Island, and (the agent being absent,) told the interpreter what I wanted to say to these people, viz: "Not to settle on

[1] Rock River and the Mississippi River.
[2] Alluvial soil on the margin of a river.
[3] The summer of 1819, apparently. [Footnote from original document.]
[4] Thomas Forsyth, a trusted Indian agent.

our lands—nor trouble our lodges or fences—that there was plenty of land in the country for them to settle upon—and they must leave our village, as we were coming back to it in the spring." The interpreter wrote me a paper, and I went back to the village, and showed it to the intruders, but could not understand their reply. I expected, however, that they would remove, as I requested them. . . .

I returned to my hunting ground, after an absence of one moon, and related what I had done. In a short time we came up to our village, and found that the whites had not left it—but that others had come, and that the greater part of our corn-fields had been enclosed. When we landed, the whites appeared displeased because we came back. We repaired the lodges that had been left standing, and built others. . . .

My reason teaches me that *land cannot be sold.* The Great Spirit gave it to his children to live upon, and cultivate as far as is necessary for their subsistence; and so long as they occupy and cultivate it, they have the right to the soil—but if they voluntarily leave it, then any other people have a right to settle upon it. Nothing can be sold but such things as can be carried away.

In consequence of the improvements of the intruders on our fields, we found considerable difficulty to get ground to plant a little corn. Some of the whites permitted us to plant small patches in the fields they had fenced, keeping all the best ground for themselves. Our women had great difficulty in climbing their fences, (being unaccustomed to the kind,) and were ill-treated if they left a rail down.

One of my old friends thought he was safe. His corn-field was on a small island of Rock river. He planted his corn; it came up well—but the white man saw it!—he wanted the island, and took his teams over, ploughed up the corn, and re-planted it for himself! The old man shed tears; not for himself but the distress his family would be in if they raised no corn. . . .

We acquainted our agent daily with our situation, and through him, the great chief[5] at St. Louis—and hoped that something would be done for us. The whites were *complaining* at the same time that *we* were *intruding* upon *their rights!* THEY made themselves out the *injured* party, and *we* the *intruders!* And called loudly to the great war chief to protect *their* property.

How smooth must be the language of the whites, when they can make right look like wrong, and wrong like right.

[5] This was General Wm. Clark of Lewis and Clark fame, who had general administrative control of the tribes [in the region]. [Footnote from original document.]

12

Memorial and Protest of the Cherokee Nation
June 22, 1836

According to the U.S. Constitution, Indian tribes are entitled to the protection of the federal government. Unfortunately, western expansion placed the interests of Indian peoples and white settlers at odds. Until the 1820s, the federal government generally made a good-faith effort to annex Native Americans' land through legally negotiated treaties drawn up with the consent of tribal members.

The election of Andrew Jackson as president in 1828 led to an aggressive shift in Indian policy (see Document 10). In the wake of the 1830 Indian Removal Act, intense pressure was placed on the tribes to cede their land. The Cherokees, the most "civilized" of the tribes, held firm. They appealed to the U.S. Supreme Court, which upheld their right to their land in 1831 and 1832. In 1835, however, a splinter group of Cherokees signed a federal treaty agreeing to move. Although the tribe loudly disavowed the treaty and Andrew Jackson was aware that it was illegitimate, it provided the justification for forcing the Cherokees to move.

The following selection is part of a protest submitted by Cherokee leaders to Congress in 1836—one of dozens they sent in a desperate attempt to retain their land. The Cherokees hoped to sway public opinion by demonstrating both their "civilization" and the obvious unfairness of their treatment. Whereas Black Hawk explicitly contrasted the ethics and beliefs of his tribe with that of whites to prove that the Sacs and Foxes had been cheated out of their land (see Document 11), the Cherokees here take a different tack, focusing on European concepts of treaties and laws. Note how they use the same language of "savagery" that Jackson does in Document 10.

This document was received by Congress and published in newspapers sympathetic to the tribe. The excerpt here is from The Friend, *a Philadelphia newspaper directed to Quakers, a pacifist religious sect that opposed slavery and Indian removal. Unfortunately, Cherokee efforts to retain their land failed. The vast majority of Cherokees were forced to move to Indian Territory (now Oklahoma) along what became known as the*

From "Memorial and Protest of the Cherokee Nation," in *The Friend: A Religious and Literary Journal*, ed. Robert Smith (Philadelphia: Adam Waldie, 1836), 9:359–60.

Trail of Tears in 1838 and 1839. At least four thousand Cherokees died along the way.

It would be useless to recapitulate the numerous provisions for the security and protection of the rights of the Cherokees, to be found in the various treaties between their nation and the United States. The Cherokees were happy and prosperous under a scrupulous observance of treaty stipulations by the government of the United States, and, from the fostering hand extended over them, they made rapid advances in civilization, morals, and in the arts and sciences. Little did they anticipate, that when taught to think and feel as the American citizen, and to have with him a common interest, they were to be *despoiled by their guardian*, to become strangers and wanderers in the land of their fathers, forced to return to the savage life, and to seek a new home in the wilds of the far west, and that without their consent. An instrument purporting to be a treaty with the Cherokee people, has recently been made public by the president of the United States, that will have such an operation, if carried into effect. This instrument, the delegation aver before the civilized world, and in the presence of Almighty God, is fraudulent, false upon its face, made by unauthorized individuals, without the sanction, and against the wishes, of the great body of the Cherokee people. Upwards of fifteen thousand of those people have protested against it, solemnly declaring they will never acquiesce. The delegation would respectfully call the attention of your honourable body to their memorial and protest, with the accompanying documents, submitted to the senate of the United States, on the subject of the alleged treaty, which are herewith transmitted.

. . . If treaties are to be thus made and enforced, deceptive to the Indians and to the world, purporting to be a contract, when, in truth, wanting the assent of one of the pretended parties, what security would there be for any nation or tribe to retain confidence in the United States? If interest or policy require that the Cherokees be removed, without their consent, from their lands, surely the president and senate have no constitutional power to accomplish that object. They cannot do it under the power to make treaties, which are contracts, not rules prescribed by a superior, and therefore binding only by the assent of the parties. In the present instance, the assent of the Cherokee nation has not been given, but expressly denied. . . . It is the expressed wish of the government of the United States to remove the Cherokees to a place west of the Mississippi. That wish is said to be founded in humanity to the Indians. To make their situation more comfortable, and to preserve them as a distinct people. Let facts show how this *benevolent* design has been prosecuted, and how faithfully to the spirit and letter has the promise of the president of the United States to the Cherokees been fulfilled — that *"those who remain may be assured of our patronage, our aid, and good neighbourhood."* The delegation are not deceived by empty professions, and fear their race is to be destroyed by the mercenary policy of the present day, and their lands wrested from them by physical force.

13

LYMAN BEECHER

A Plea for the West

1835

The conviction that Americans were destined to bring enlightenment to the West was a key element of Manifest Destiny. For many American Protestants, the West was not simply a land of economic opportunity; it was also a grand stage for the religious conversion of heathen residents. Catholics were a larger and more immediate target than Native Americans. The French settlers of Canada and the Mississippi River valley were Catholic, and Catholicism was the official religion of Mexico.

The Protestant sense of religious mission became particularly acute in the aftermath of the religious revivals of the 1820s and 1830s that are collectively known as the Second Great Awakening. American anti-Catholicism arrived with the earliest settlers, but the increasing Catholic immigration of the 1830s and 1840s greatly exacerbated nativist (anti-immigrant) sentiment. The Presbyterian clergyman Lyman Beecher was one of America's best-known ministers and a central figure in the Second Great Awakening. Beecher was also violently anti-Catholic. Like many other American Protestants, he hoped to limit Catholic immigration in large part because he believed that Catholic voters were under the sway of a European Catholic conspiracy to undermine American freedom.

From Lyman Beecher, *A Plea for the West*, 2nd ed. (Cincinnati: Truman and Smith, 1835), 11–12, 31–32, 51–52, 72–73, 117–18.

Beecher was convinced that a struggle between Catholics and Prot-estants was inevitable and would take place in the American West. He became president of Lane Theological Seminary in Cincinnati (then considered a "western" city) to train Protestant clergymen to fight the Catholic menace in their backyard. Beecher delivered versions of the speech excerpted here in cities across the Northeast in 1834 as he at-tempted to raise money for Lane and other Protestant institutions in the trans-Appalachian West. Beecher's view of the West as ground zero in the coming struggle with Catholicism reflects the importance the region held in the Protestant imagination and the way American Protestants regarded the residents of Mexico on the eve of the Texas Revolution.

If this nation is, in the providence of God, destined to lead the way in the moral and political emancipation of the world, it is time she understood her high calling, and were harnessed for the work. . . .

It is equally plain that the religious and political destiny of our nation is to be decided in the West. There is the territory, and there soon will be the population, the wealth, and the political power. The Atlantic commerce and manufactures may confer always some peculiar advantages on the East. But the West is destined to be the great central power of the nation, and under heaven, must affect powerfully the cause of free institutions and the liberty of the world.

The West is a young empire of mind, and power, and wealth, and free institutions, rushing up to a giant manhood, with a rapidity and a power never before witnessed below the sun. And if she carries with her the elements of her preservation, the experiment will be glorious—the joy of the nation—the joy of the whole earth, as she rises in the majesty of her intelligence and benevolence, and enterprise, for the emancipation of the world.

It is equally clear, that the conflict which is to decide the destiny of the West, will be a conflict of institutions for the education of her sons, for purposes of superstition, or evangelical light; of despotism, or liberty. . . .

We must educate! We must educate! or we must perish by our own prosperity. If we do not, short from the cradle to the grave will be our race. . . . And let no man at the East quiet himself, and dream of liberty, whatever may become of the West. Our alliance of blood, and political institutions, and common interests, is such, that we cannot stand aloof in the hour of her calamity, should it ever come. Her destiny is our destiny; and the day that her gallant ship goes down, our little boat sinks in the vortex! . . .

. . . Danger . . . is augmenting daily by the rapid influx of foreign emigrants, the greater part unacquainted with our institutions, unaccustomed to self-government, inaccessible to education, and easily accessible to prepossession, and inveterate credulity, and intrigue, and easily embodied and wielded by sinister design. In the beginning this eruption of revolutionary Europe was not anticipated, and we opened our doors wide to the influx and naturalization of foreigners. But it is becoming a terrific inundation; it has increased upon our native population from five to thirty-seven per cent; and is every year advancing. It seeks, of course, to settle down upon the unoccupied territory of the West, and may at no distant day equal, and even outnumber the native population. What is to be done to educate the millions which in twenty years Europe will pour out upon us? . . .

. . . Since the irruption of the northern barbarians, the world has never witnessed such a rush of dark-minded population from one country to another, as is now leaving Europe, and dashing upon our shores. It is not the *northern* hive, but the *whole* hive which is swarming out upon our cities and unoccupied territory as the effect of overstocked population, of civil oppression, of crime and poverty, and political and ecclesiastical design. Clouds like the locusts of Egypt are rising from the hills and plains of Europe, and on the wings of every wind, are coming over to settle down upon our fair fields; while millions, moved by the noise of their rising and cheered by the news of their safe arrival and green pastures, are preparing for flight in an endless succession.

Capitalists and landholders, who feel in Europe the premonitions of coming evil are transferring their treasures to our funds, and making large investments in land, and facilitating emigration to augment the value of their property. Our unoccupied soil is coming fast into the European market, and foreign capitalists and speculators are holding competition with our own. . . .

. . . "The spirit of the age" . . . is moving on to put an end in Europe to Catholic domination, creating the necessity of making reprisals abroad for what liberty conquers at home. Their policy points them to the West, the destined centre of civilization and political power once their own, and embracing now their ancient settlements and institutions and people, and not a little wealth — bounded on the north by a Catholic population, and on the south by a continent not yet emancipated from

their dominion, and agitated by the at present successful conflicts of
the Catholic priesthood to extinguish free institutions and reconstruct
those of despotic power.

14

HARRIET MARTINEAU

On Land-Lust in America

1837

*Harriet Martineau, a respected British journalist and political reformer,
was thirty-two years old when she embarked on a tour of the United
States. Like other European intellectuals in the 1830s, she was intrigued
by the dramatic economic development and social change in the United
States, and she crossed the Atlantic with the goal of informing her country
about events in America. Martineau spent two years traveling around the
United States and attempted to evaluate what she saw objectively, without
applying British norms to her account. While she had only praise for
American democracy, she was open in her criticism of the inequality that
economic development had fostered.*

*Martineau produced three books about American society, all of which
were favorably received in Britain. In the United States, however, her
open support of woman's rights and the abolitionist movement led to
widespread condemnation. The careful observational methodology that
she cultivated in these volumes proved a forerunner of modern sociology.
In this excerpt, drawn from a chapter on agriculture in her 1837 volume,
Martineau discusses the meaning of land to Americans, as Manifest Destiny
became a driving force in expansionism. She provides an explanation
for why so many Americans were willing to undergo intense hardships in
order to gain new land for themselves and their families.*

From Harriet Martineau, *Society in America* (New York: Unders and Otley, 1837),
1:291–93.

The pride and delight of Americans is in their quantity of land. I do not remember meeting with one to whom it had occurred that they had too much. Among the many complaints of the minority, this was never one. I saw a gentleman strike his fist on the table in an agony at the country being so "confoundedly prosperous": I heard lamentations over the spirit of speculation; the migration of young men to the back country; the fluctuating state of society from the incessant movement westwards; the immigration of labourers from Europe; and the ignorance of the sparse population. All these grievances I heard perpetually complained of; but in the same breath I was told in triumph of the rapid sales of land; of the glorious additions which had been made by the acquisition of Louisiana and Florida, and of the probable gain of Texas. Land was spoken of as the unfailing resource against over manufacture;[1] the great wealth of the nation; the grand security of every man in it. . . .

The possession of land is the aim of all action, generally speaking, and the cure for all social evils, among men in the United States. If a man is disappointed in politics or love, he goes and buys land. If he disgraces himself, he betakes himself to a lot in the west. If the demand for any article of manufacture slackens, the operatives drop into the unsettled lands. If a citizen's neighbours rise above him in the towns, he betakes himself where he can be monarch of all he surveys. An artisan works, that he may die on land of his own. He is frugal, that he may enable his son to be a landowner. Farmers' daughters go into factories that they may clear off the mortgage from their fathers' farms; that they may be independent landowners again. All this is natural enough in a country colonised from an old one, where land is so restricted in quantity as to be apparently the same thing as wealth. It is natural enough in a young republic, where independence is of the highest political value.

---

[1] An economy's excessive reliance on manufacturing.

15

PATHIÑ-NAÑPAJI

An Encounter between Omaha Hunters and White Squatters in Iowa
1853

The conflict described here between hunters of the Omaha tribe and Mormon squatters in western Iowa near the Nebraska border took place in 1853, but it represents countless other encounters between whites and Indians in the nineteenth century. As whites moved west, settling on land to which they had no legal title, they frequently invaded Native American hunting grounds. While Indians and whites had dramatically different conceptions of landownership (see Document 11), the conversation recounted here between an Omaha hunter and a white squatter reveals the extent to which both parties understood the legal status of the land in question, as well as the likely fate of such land. This account was provided to the anthropologist and linguist James Owen Dorsey between 1878 and 1880 by an elderly Omaha warrior named Pathiñ-nañpaji (He Who Fears Not a Pawnee When He Sees Him).

We killed deer when we went on the autumnal hunt. We hunted all sorts of small leaping animals. When we approached any place to pitch the tents, we were in excellent spirits. Day after day we carried into camp different animals, such as deer, raccoons, badgers, skunks, and wild turkeys. We had ten lodges in our party. As we went, we camped for the night. And we camped again at night, being in excellent spirits. At length we reached a place where some white farmers dwelt. They gave us food, which was very good. At length they assembled us. "Come, ye Indians, we must talk together. Let us talk to each other at night." "Yes," said we. As they came for us when a part of the night had passed, we said, "Let us go." They came with us to a very large house. Behold, all of the whites had arrived. That place was beyond the Little Sioux River, at Boyer Creek, where the first white men were, across the country from

---

From James Owen Dorsey, *The Cegiha Language* (Washington, D.C.: Government Printing Office, 1890), 447–48.

this place. They talked with us. "Oho! my friends, though I, for my part, talk with you, you will do just what I say," said one. "We will consider it. If it be good, we will do so," said the Omahas. "I am unwilling for you to wander over this land," said the white man. ᶫe-saⁿ (White-Buffalo-in-the-distance) said, "As you keep all your stock at home, you have no occasion to wander in search of them; and you dwell nowhere else but at this place. (But we have wild animals, which are beyond our dwelling-place, though they are on our land.)" "Though you say so, the land is mine," said the white man. "The land is not yours. The President did not buy it. You have jumped on it. You know that the President has not bought it, and I know it full well," said ᶫe-saⁿ. "If the President bought it, are you so intelligent that you would know about it?" said the white man, speaking in a sneering manner to the Omaha. ᶫe-saⁿ hit the white man several times on the chest. "Why do you consider me a fool? You are now dwelling a little beyond the bounds of the land belonging to the President. It is through me that you shall make yourself a person (*i.e.*, you shall improve your condition at my expense). I wish to eat my animals that grow of their own accord, so I walk seeking them," said ᶫe-saⁿ. "Nevertheless, I am unwilling. If you go further, instead of obeying my words, we shall fight," said the white man. "I will go beyond. You may fight me. As the land is mine, I shall go," said ᶫe-saⁿ. "Yes, if you go to-morrow, I will go to you to see you. I shall collect the young white people all around, and go with them to see you," said the white man. Having removed the camp in the morning, we scattered to hunt for game. I went with three men. About forty white men arrived, and stood there to intercept us. They waved their hands at us, saying, "Do not come any further." As we still went on, they came with a rush, and tried to snatch our guns from us. When we refused to let them go, they shot at us: "Ku! ku! ku!" As we went back, we were driven towards the rest of our party. The leader of the white men said, "Do not go. If you go, I will shoot at you." We stood on an island; and the white men surrounded us. "You have already shot at us," said the Omahas. The white men doubted their word, saying, "It is not so about us." "You have already shot at us, so we will go at all hazards. I am following my trail in my own land. I am going to hunt. Why do you behave so? Make way for us. We will go to you," said ᶫe-saⁿ. "If you speak saucily to me, I will shoot at you," said the white man. "Ho! If you wish to do that, do it," said the Omahas. As they departed, the whites made way for them. We went along a bluff, and then down-hill, when we reached a creek. It was a good place for us to stay, so we remained there.

At length about two hundred white men came in sight. We were just thirty. We were in the hollow by the edge of the stream. Wanace-jiñga, whom I have spoken of, arrived in sight. He looked at them. When he made a sudden signal, he was wounded in the arm. "They have wounded me! There is cause for anger! They have wounded me severely," said he. "Oho! come, let us attack them at any rate," said the Omahas. We all stood, and gave the scalp yell. Having formed a line, we went to attack them. We scared off the white men. All of them were mounted; but only one Omaha, Agaha-ma^n¢i^n, was on a horse. He rode round and round, and gave us directions what to do. "Miss in firing at the white men. Shoot elsewhere every time," said he. At length the Omahas intercepted the retreat of the whites. "Come, stop pursuing. Let us cease. It is good not to injure even one of the white people, who are our own flesh and blood," said Agaha-ma^n¢i^n.

16

ZENAS LEONARD

A Fur Trapper's View of Manifest Destiny
1839

Zenas Leonard, a farm boy raised in the Allegheny Mountains of central Pennsylvania, joined a Rocky Mountain fur-trapping company in 1831 at age twenty-two. In 1833 he signed on with an expedition traveling to the Pacific, crossed the salt flats of Utah, fought the Paiutes of Nevada, and nearly perished crossing the Sierra Nevada. The expedition has been credited as the first to visit Yosemite Valley. After four years of hardship, Leonard returned home to Pennsylvania with little money but many tales of adventure. He published an account of his experiences in serial form in his hometown newspaper in 1838–1839 and, due to popular demand, in book form in 1839. Narratives of exploration like Leonard's were popular in the United States during the first half of the nineteenth century and

From Zenas Leonard, *Leonard's Narrative: Adventures of Zenas Leonard, Fur Trader and Trapper, 1831–1836*, ed. William Finley Wagner (1839; repr., Cleveland: Burrows Brothers, 1904), 192–93.

*acquainted American readers with new, unsettled regions that might
become subject to the nation's Manifest Destiny.*

*This selection follows Leonard's description of northern California.
Although he asserts that the land west of the Sierra Nevada belonged "to
the Republic of the United States," in fact the area lay entirely within
Mexico's province of Alta California. Oregon, hundreds of miles to the
north, was jointly controlled by the United States and Britain at the time.
Leonard seems either unaware of or uninterested in these details. Rather,
he is concerned with who is entitled to it — that is, those putting it to
proper use.*

Most of this vast waste of territory belongs to the Republic of the United
States. What a theme to contemplate its settlement and civilization. Will
the jurisdiction of the federal government ever succeed in civilizing the
thousands of savages now roaming over these plains, and her hardy
freeborn population here plant their homes, build their towns and cities, and say here shall the arts and sciences of civilization take root and
flourish? yes, here, even in this remote part of the great west before
many years, will these hills and valleys be greeted with the enlivening
sound, of the workman's hammer, and the merry whistle of the plough-
boy. But this is left undone by the government, and will only be seen
when too late to apply the remedy. The Spaniards are making inroads
on the South — the Russians are encroaching with impunity along the
sea shore to the North, and further North-east the British are pushing
their stations into the very heart of our territory, which, even at this
day, more resemble military forts to resist invasion, than trading stations. Our government should be vigilant. She should assert her claim
by taking possession of the whole territory as soon as possible — for we
have good reason to suppose that the territory *west* of the mountain[1]
will some day be equally as important to the nation as that on the *east*.

[1] The Sierra Nevada.

17

UNITED STATES DEMOCRATIC REVIEW

The Great Nation of Futurity

November 1839

American writers from the seventeenth century onward asserted that their "citty upon a hill" was unique in history, exceptionally virtuous, and destined by God to spread in both territory and influence. In 1839 an unidentified writer working for the United States Democratic Review *placed this exceptionalist worldview at the heart of an article announcing the doctrine of Manifest Destiny to the world.*

The identity of the author of "The Great Nation of Futurity" has been contested. Democratic Review *editor John L. O'Sullivan was long assumed to have written this piece and thus to have first introduced* Manifest Destiny. *But scholars have recently suggested that Jane McManus Storm Cazneau, a writer for the journal who used the pen name Cora Montgomery, may have been the actual author. There were very few female political writers in the era of Manifest Destiny, since politics was considered inappropriate subject matter for women to address. But Montgomery was in many ways as exceptional as the great nation of the future discussed here because she was an active proponent of U.S. expansion into Mexico and the Caribbean. Note the dramatic ambitions the author holds for U.S. territorial expansion.*

The American people having derived their origin from many other nations, and the Declaration of National Independence being entirely based on the great principle of human equality, these facts demonstrate at once our disconnected position as regards any other nation; that we have, in reality, but little connection with the past history of any of them, and still less with all antiquity, its glories, or its crimes. On the contrary, our national birth was the beginning of a new history, the formation and progress of an untried political system, which separates us from the past and connects us with the future only; and so far as regards the entire development of the natural rights of man, in moral, political, and

From "The Great Nation of Futurity," in *United States Magazine and Democratic Review* (Washington, D.C.: Langtree and O'Sullivan, 1839), 6:426–27.

national life, we may confidently assume that our country is destined to be *the great nation* of futurity. . . .

We have no interest in the scenes of antiquity, only as lessons of avoidance of nearly all their examples. The expansive future is our arena, and for our history. We are entering on its untrodden space, with the truths of God in our minds, beneficent objects in our hearts, and with a clear conscience unsullied by the past. We are the nation of human progress, and who will, what can, set limits to our onward march? . . .

The far-reaching, the boundless future will be the era of American greatness. In its magnificent domain of space and time, the nation of many nations is destined to manifest to mankind the excellence of divine principles; to establish on earth the noblest temple ever dedicated to the worship of the Most High—the Sacred and the True. Its floor shall be a hemisphere—its roof the firmament of the star-studded heavens, and its congregation an Union of many Republics, comprising hundreds of happy millions, calling, owning no man master, but governed by God's natural and moral law of equality, the law of brotherhood—of "peace and good will amongst men."

18

RICHARD HENRY DANA

Two Years before the Mast

1840

Richard Henry Dana was, like Zenas Leonard (see Document 16), a northerner who explored the Pacific coast in the 1830s and wrote about his adventures with a clear faith in America's Manifest Destiny. But the similarities end there. Dana, a wealthy Bostonian of Puritan ancestry, left Harvard College to enlist as a merchant seaman at age nineteen in the hope that time afloat would improve his ill health. He spent two years at sea, visiting Mexican ports along the Pacific coast, including California, and published his account of the trip in 1840. Dana's elegant writing style and rhapsodic prose won acclaim. His racist view of Mexicans and

From Richard Henry Dana, *Two Years before the Mast* (New York: Harper and Brothers, 1841), 212, 214–16.

critique of their political and social systems also offered an implicit jus-
tification for the U.S. conquest of California. When gold was discovered
there, the book became a bestseller, and gold rush pioneers used it as a
travel guide. In this excerpt, taken from a chapter titled "California and
Its Inhabitants," Dana offers his views of California society and the future
of the region.

Revolutions are matters of constant occurrence in California. They are
got up by men who are at the foot of the ladder and in desperate circumstances, just as a new political party is started by such men in our own
country. The only object, of course, is the loaves and fishes;[1] and instead
of caucusing, paragraphing, libelling, feasting, promising, and lying, as
with us, they take muskets and bayonets, and seizing upon the presidio
and custom-house, divide the spoils, and declare a new dynasty. As for
justice, they know no law but will and fear. . . .

In their domestic relations, these people are no better than in their
public. The men are thriftless, proud, and extravagant, and very much
given to gaming; and the women have but little education, and a good
deal of beauty, and their morality, of course, is none of the best; yet the
instances of infidelity are much less frequent than one would at first suppose. In fact, one vice is set over against another; and thus, something
like a balance is obtained. The women have but little virtue, but then
the jealousy of their husbands is extreme, and their revenge deadly and
almost certain. . . .

Of the poor Indians, very little care is taken. The priests, indeed, at
the missions, are said to keep them very strictly, and some rules are usually made by the alcaldes[2] to punish their misconduct; but it all amounts
to but little. Indeed, to show the entire want of any sense of morality
or domestic duty among them, I have frequently known an Indian to
bring his wife, to whom he was lawfully married in the church, down
to the beach, and carry her back again, dividing with her the money
which she had got from the sailors. If any of the girls were discovered
by the alcalde to be open evil-livers, they were whipped, and kept at
work sweeping the square of the presidio, and carrying mud and bricks
for the buildings; yet a few reáls would generally buy them off. Intem-
perance, too, is a common vice among the Indians. The Spaniards, on

---

[1] Allegedly feeding the multitude. Dana is sarcastic here.
[2] Magistrates or judges.

the contrary, are very abstemious, and I do not remember ever having
seen a Spaniard intoxicated.

Such are the people who inhabit a country embracing four or five
hundred miles of sea-coast, with several good harbors; with fine forests in the north; the waters filled with fish, and the plains covered with
thousands of herds of cattle; blessed with a climate, than which there
can be no better in the world; free from all manner of diseases, whether
epidemic or endemic; and with a soil in which corn yields from seventy
to eighty fold. In the hands of an enterprising people, what a country
this might be! we are ready to say. Yet how long would a people remain
so, in such a country? The Americans (as those from the United States
are called) and Englishmen, who are fast filling up the principal towns,
and getting the trade into their hands, are indeed more industrious and
effective than the Spaniards; yet their children are brought up Spaniards, in every respect, and if the "California fever" (laziness) spares the
first generation, it always attacks the second.

19

RALPH WALDO EMERSON

The Young American

1844

*Ralph Waldo Emerson of Concord, Massachusetts, was one of America's
great philosophers. He was also the father of transcendentalism, an
antebellum philosophical movement that promoted individual intuition,
rather than religious doctrine, as the key to both personal and social
enlightenment. In 1844, when he first delivered his lecture "The Young
American" before the Mercantile Library Association of Boston, he was
already a much-acclaimed essayist and orator whose profound, highly
intellectual lectures attracted large and enthusiastic crowds of middle-
class Americans.*

*Although Emerson asked listeners to cultivate self-reliance, reject mate-
rialism, and ignore the views of others (all tenets of transcendentalism),*

From Ralph Waldo Emerson, "The Young American," in *Essays, Orations, and Lectures*
(London: William Tegg, 1848), 154, 169.

*his highly abstract oratory and use of elaborate metaphors led to his being
frequently misunderstood by his audiences. There is no evidence that
Emerson intended to advocate in favor of Manifest Destiny in this speech,
and he became an outspoken opponent of the U.S.-Mexican War in 1846.
But "The Young American" appeared to offer a "call to arms" to young
men to aspire to greatness, while at the same time advocating in favor of
a near-boundless natural future with a clearly western focus. This lecture
proved so inspirational to Democratic expansionists that they adopted the
name Young America for their movement.*

The bountiful continent is ours, state on state, and territory on territory,
to the waves of the Pacific sea: —

> "Our garden is the immeasurable earth,
> The heaven's blue pillars are Medea's house,"

and new duties, new motives, await and cheer us. The task of planting,
of surveying, of building upon this immense tract, requires an education
and a sentiment commensurate thereto. A consciousness of this fact is
beginning to take the place of the purely trading spirit and education
which sprang up whilst all the population lived on the fringe of sea-coast.
And even on the coast, prudent men have begun to see that every American should be educated with a view to the values of land. The arts of
engineering and of architecture are studied; scientific agriculture is an
object of growing attention; the mineral riches are explored; limestone,
coal, slate, and iron; and the value of timberlands is enhanced.

Columbus alleged as a reason for seeking a continent in the West, that
the harmony of nature required a great tract of land in the western hemisphere, to balance the known extent of land in the eastern; and it now
appears that we must estimate the native values of this immense region
to redress the balance of our own judgment, and appreciate the advantages opened to the human race in this country, which is our fortunate
home. The land is the appointed remedy for whatever is false and fantastic in our culture. The great continent we inhabit is to be physic and
food for our mind, as well as our body. The land, with its tranquillizing,
sanative influences, is to repair the errors of a scholastic and traditional
education, and bring us into just relations with men and things. . . .

I call upon you, young men, to obey your heart, and be the nobility
of this land. In every age of the world, there has been a leading nation,

one of a more generous sentiment, whose eminent citizens were willing to stand for the interests of general justice and humanity, at the risk of being called, by the men of the moment, chimerical and fantastic. Which should be that nation but these States? Which should lead that movement, if not New England? Who should lead the leaders but the young American? The people, and the world, is now suffering from the want of religion and honour in its public mind. In America, out of doors all seems a market; in doors, an air-tight stove of conventionalism. Everybody who comes into our houses savours of these precious habits: the men of the market, the women of the custom. I find no expression in our state papers or legislative debate, in our lyceums or churches, specially in our newspapers, of a high national feeling, no lofty counsels that rightfully stir the blood. . . . But who announces to us in journal, or in pulpit, or in the street,

> "Man alone
> Can perform the impossible."

4

Texas and Oregon

20

MANUEL MIER Y TERÁN

Letter to President Guadalupe Victoria

June 30, 1828

In 1824 the government of newly independent Mexico made a serious error when it invited immigrants to settle in the state of Coahuila and Texas on Mexico's northern frontier. Mexico believed that increased settlement would improve the economic and social conditions of the underpopulated territory. Lured by extremely cheap land prices, American settlers flocked to the region and quickly became a problem. They almost immediately outnumbered Spanish-speaking Texans (Tejanos) in the northern part of the state. Although all settlers had to take an oath of allegiance to Mexico, the Americans chafed under their lack of legal and political representation. In the mid 1820s both the state and federal government moved to end slavery, though most of the American settlers continued to own slaves.

In late 1827, President Guadalupe Victoria ordered General Manuel Mier y Terán, the commander general of the region, to investigate conditions in Texas. Terán arrived in Béjar (now San Antonio) on March 10, 1828. He traveled the Texas countryside for three months, meeting with both American and Mexican settlers. Concerned about the future of the territory, he sent the following private letter to President Victoria from Nacogdoches, in what is today eastern Texas, on June 30, 1828. A year later, he submitted a formal report to Mexico's war department expressing a similarly pessimistic view of the country's hold on Texas. Note his

From Alleine Howren, "Causes and Origin of the Decree of April 6, 1830," *Southwestern Historical Quarterly* 16 (April 1913): 395–96.

evaluation of the relative virtues of Mexican and American residents and what he sees as the potential growth of Texas should slavery become legal.

As one covers the distance from Béjar to this town,[1] he will note that Mexican influence is proportionately diminished until on arriving in this place he will see that it is almost nothing. And indeed, whence could such influence come? Hardly from superior numbers in population, since the ratio of Mexicans to foreigners is one to ten; certainly not from the superior character of the Mexican population, for exactly the opposite is true, the Mexicans of this town comprising what in all countries is called the lowest class—the very poor and very ignorant. The naturalized North Americans in the town maintain an English school, and send their children north for further education; the poor Mexicans not only do not have sufficient means to establish schools, but they are not of the type that take any thought for the improvement of its public institutions or the betterment of its degraded condition. Neither are there civil authorities or magistrates; . . . yet, wherever I have looked, in the short time that I have been here, I have witnessed grave occurrences, both political and judicial. It would cause you the same chagrin that it has caused me to see the opinion that is held of our nation by these foreign colonists, since, with the exception of some few who have journeyed to our capital, they know no other Mexicans than the inhabitants about here, and excepting the authorities necessary to any form of society, the said inhabitants are the most ignorant of negroes and Indians, among whom I pass for a man of culture. Thus, I tell myself that it could not be otherwise than that from such a state of affairs should arise an antagonism between the Mexicans and foreigners, which is not the least of the smoldering fires which I have discovered. Therefore, I am warning you to take timely measures. Texas could throw the whole nation into revolution.

The colonists murmur against the political disorganization of the frontier, and the Mexicans complain of the superiority and better education of the colonists; the colonists find it unendurable that they must go three hundred leagues to lodge a complaint against the petty pickpocketing that they suffer from a venal and ignorant *alcalde.* . . . Meanwhile, the incoming stream of new settlers is unceasing; the first news of these comes by discovering them on land already under cultivation, where they have been located for many months; the old inhabitants set

[1] Nacogdoches, approximately three hundred miles from Béjar.

up a claim to the property, basing their titles of doubtful priority, and for which there are no records, on a law of the Spanish government; and thus arises a lawsuit in which the *alcalde* has a chance to come out with some money. In this state of affairs, the town where there are no magistrates is the one in which lawsuits abound, and it is at once evident that in Nacogdoches and its vicinity, being most distant from the seat of the general government, the primitive order of things should take its course, which is to say that this section is being settled up without the consent of anybody.

The majority of the North Americans established here under the Spanish government—and these are few—are of two classes. First, those who are fugitives from our neighbor republic and bear the unmistakable earmarks of thieves and criminals; these are located between Nacogdoches and the Sabine, ready to cross and recross this river as they see the necessity of separating themselves from the country in which they have just committed some crime; however, some of these have reformed and settled down to an industrious life in the new country. The other class of early settlers are poor laborers who lack the four or five thousand dollars necessary to buy a *sitio* [4,428 acres] of land in the north, but having the ambition to become landholders—one of the strong virtues of our neighbors—have come to Texas. Of such as this latter class is Austin's colony composed. They are for the most part industrious and honest, and appreciate this country. Most of them own at least one or two slaves. Unfortunately the emigration of such is made under difficulties, because they lack the means of transportation, and to accomplish this emigration it has become necessary to do what was not necessary until lately: there are empresarios of wealth who advance them the means for their transportation and establishment.

The wealthy Americans of Louisiana and other western states are anxious to secure land in Texas for speculation, but they are restrained by the laws prohibiting slavery. If these laws should be repealed—which God forbid—in a few years Texas would be a powerful state which could compete in productions and wealth with Louisiana.

21

ROBERT J. WALKER

Letter in Favor of the Reannexation of Texas

January 8, 1844

Robert J. Walker was a Democratic politician and lawyer from Pennsylvania who moved to Mississippi in his twenties and quickly established himself as a wealthy slave-owning planter on land taken from the Choctaws in 1830. Elected to represent Mississippi in the U.S. Senate in 1836, Walker became a strong advocate for the rights of southerners, although he also knew how to appeal to northerners. This letter was written at the height of the controversy over whether to annex Texas. Interestingly, this appeal took the form of a letter to supporters in Kentucky, although it was actually intended for publication in the North. Most of the arguments were written to persuade northerners that the admission of another slave state would not harm their interests. Walker appealed to northern racism, as well as to Anglophobia (anti-British sentiment, which was widespread in the United States) and concerns about national security. He also made the somewhat disingenuous claim that Texas was within the boundaries of the Louisiana Purchase and wrongly transferred to Spain in the Adams-Onís Treaty of 1819.

Walker's letter proved influential. Whether or not northerners accepted his reasoning, his views were parroted by countless politicians and journalists who supported the annexation of Texas. In part to thank Walker for his efforts in advancing the cause of annexation, President James K. Polk appointed him secretary of the treasury in 1845.

Walker, like any number of other outspoken advocates of expansionism, had a financial interest in the annexation of Texas. Both he and members of his family had speculated in land there.

The treaty by which Texas was surrendered to Spain, was always opposed by me; and in 1826, 1834, and 1835, various addresses were made by me, and then published, in favour of the reannexation of Texas;

From Robert J. Walker, *Letter of Mr. Walker, of Mississippi, Relative to the Reannexation of Texas: In Reply to the Call of the People of Carroll County, Kentucky, to Communicate His Views on That Subject* (Philadelphia: Mifflin and Parry, 1844), 3, 15.

and the same opinions have been often expressed by me since my election, in 1836, to the Senate of the Union.

It was a revolution in Mexico that produced the conflict for independence in Texas. The citizens of Texas had been invited there by Mexico, under the solemn guaranty of the federal constitution of 1824. This constitution, to which Texas so long and faithfully adhered, was prostrated by the usurper Santa Anna.[1] After a severe struggle, the people of Mexico were subdued by a mercenary army; the States were annihilated, and a military dictator was placed at the head of a central despotism. In the capital of Mexico, and of the state of Coahuila and Texas, the civil authorities were suppressed by the bayonet; the disarming of every citizen was decreed, and the soldiery of the usurper proceeded to enforce this edict. The people of Texas resolved to resist, and perish upon the field of battle, rather than submit to the despotic sway of a treacherous and sanguinary military dictator. Short was the conflict, and glorious the issue. The American race was successful; the armies of the tyrant were overthrown and dispersed, and the dictator himself was captured. He was released by Texas, and restored to his country, having first acknowledged, by a solemn treaty, the independence of Texas. . . .

. . . The question is asked, is slavery never to disappear from the Union? This is a startling and momentous question, but the answer is easy, and the proof is clear; *it will certainly disappear if Texas is reannexed to the Union*; not by abolition, but against and in spite of all its frenzy, slowly, and gradually, by diffusion, as it has already thus nearly receded from several of the more northern of the slaveholding States,[2] and as it will continue thus more rapidly to recede by the reannexation of Texas, and finally, in the distant future, without a shock, without abolition, without a convulsion, disappear into and through Texas, into Mexico and Central and Southern America. Thus, that same overruling Providence that watched over the landing of the emigrants and pilgrims at Jamestown and Plymouth; that gave us the victory in our struggle for independence; that guided by His inspiration the framers of our wonderful constitution; that has thus far preserved this great Union from dangers so many and imminent, and is now shielding it from abolition, its most dangerous and internal foe — will open Texas as a safety-valve, into and through which slavery will slowly and gradually recede, and

---

[1] General Antonio López de Santa Anna overthrew the Mexican constitution of 1824 and established a military dictatorship in Mexico.

[2] Walker is referring to the mistaken belief that slavery was dying out in the upper South in the 1840s.

finally disappear into the boundless regions of Mexico, and Central and Southern America. Beyond the Del Norte,[3] slavery will not pass; not only because it is forbidden by law, but because the coloured races there preponderate in the ratio of ten to one over the whites; and holding, as they do, the government, and most of the offices in their own possession, they will never permit the enslavement of any portion of the coloured race which makes and executes the laws of the country. . . .

The outlet for our negro race, through this vast region, can never be opened but by the reannexation of Texas; but in that event, there, in that extensive country, bordering upon our negro population, and four times greater in area than the whole Union, with a sparse population of but three to the square mile, where nine-tenths of the population is of the coloured races, there, upon that fertile soil, and in that delicious climate, so admirably adapted to the negro race, as all experience has now clearly proved, the free black would find a home. There, also, as slaves, in the lapse of time, from the density of population and other causes, are emancipated, they will disappear from time to time west of the Del Norte, and beyond the limits of the Union, among a race of their own colour; will be diffused throughout this vast region, where they will not be a degraded caste, and where, as to climate, and social and moral condition, and all the hopes and comforts of life, they can occupy, among equals, a position they can never attain in any part of this Union.

The reannexation of Texas would strengthen and fortify the whole Union, and antedate the period when our own country would be the first and greatest of all the powers of the earth. To the South and Southwest it would give peace and security; to agriculture and manufactures, to the products of the mines, the forest, and fisheries, new and important markets, that otherwise must soon be lost forever. To the commercial and navigating interests, it would give a new impulse; and not a canal or a railroad throughout the Union, that would not derive increased business, and augmented profits; whilst the great city of New York, the centre of most of the business of the Union, would take a mighty step in advance towards that destiny which must place her above London in wealth, in business and population. Indeed, when, as Americans, we look at the city of New York, its deep, accessible and capacious harbour, united by canals and the Hudson, with the St. Lawrence and the lakes, the Ohio, and the Mississippi, with two-thirds of the imports, and one-third of the exports of the whole Union, with all its trade, internal, coastwise, and foreign, and reflect how great and rapidly augmenting an

---

[3] Another name for the Rio Grande, at the southern border of modern Texas.

accession to its business would be made by the reannexation of Texas; and know that, by the failure of this measure, what is lost to us is gained by England, can we hesitate, or do we never wish to see the day when New York shall take from London the trident of the ocean, and the command of the commerce of the world? Or do we prefer London to New York, and England to America? And do the opponents of reannexation suppose that a British Parliament, and not an American Congress, sits in the capitol of the Union. Shall, then, Texas be our own, with all its markets, commerce, and products, or shall we drive it into the arms of England, now outstretched to receive it, and striving to direct its destiny?

22

DANIEL WEBSTER

Letter to the Citizens of Worcester County, Massachusetts

January 23, 1844

Whig senator Daniel Webster of Massachusetts was one of America's most respected politicians when he spoke out against territorial expansion in general, and the possible annexation of Texas in particular, at the beginning of 1844. Like Federalists before them (see Document 7), Whigs were ambivalent about territorial growth from the party's origins in the 1820s until its decline in the 1850s. The Whig power base was in the Northeast and along the Atlantic coast; expansionism threatened to marginalize these regions.

Whigs pushed for the development of American industry and the construction of roads and bridges between already settled areas. They were also far more comfortable with the idea of a strong federal government than were Democrats. Democrats feared centralized power and looked to individual ownership of farms as an ideal, while Whigs had trouble imagining how a nation without territorial limits could develop its resources and hold together.

From Daniel Webster, "Letter to the Citizens of Worcester County, Massachusetts," in *The Writings and Speeches of Daniel Webster Hitherto Uncollected*, ed. Edward Everett (Boston: Little, Brown, 1903), 4:422–24.

Webster's views suggest why many Americans who shared an exceptionalist worldview still found Manifest Destiny unpersuasive. Like Robert J. Walker (see Document 21), Webster wrote a letter to supporters knowing that it would be published. That letter, excerpted here, appeared in the country's leading commercial journal, the Baltimore-based Niles' Weekly Register, *in March 1844, just weeks after Texas signed a treaty committing to annexation.*

It is not to be doubted that the continuance of the American union, and its prosperity and success, under its present form of government, is a matter of high moment to all mankind. It is one of the most cherished hopes and reliances of that universal cause of which you speak; the cause of human knowledge, virtue, liberty, and happiness. And he is a bolder reasoner than I am, who has satisfied himself that this government may be extended indefinitely either to the north or to the south, without endangering its stability and its duration.

It is true that under the beneficial operation of the practical principle of maintaining local governments for local purposes, and confiding general interests to a general government, the ends of political society are capable of being fulfilled, by the same free and popular system, and the same administration, over a large portion of the earth. This is the result of our experience; but our experience is the only instance of such a result. A monarchical and arbitrary government may extend itself to the full limit of its military means. Under such a government, society is kept together by pressure from above, by the weight of the government itself, and the strength of its arm. But how obvious is it that, in free, elective systems, the political society exists and coheres, and must exist and cohere, not by superincumbent pressure on its several parts, but by the internal and mutual attraction of those parts; by the assimilation of interests and feelings; by a sense of common country, common political family, common character, fortune and destiny. Not only the organization of such systems, but also their continuance by means of periodical popular elections; necessarily requires intercourse, mutual conference and understanding, and a general acquaintance among those who are to unite in such elections. When individuals are to be selected for high situations in government, and to exercise an influence over the happiness of all, it would seem indispensable that a general, if not a universal confidence should be inspired by knowledge of their character, their virtue and patriotism. It certainly may be very well questioned, with how much of mutual intelligence, and how much of a spirit of conciliation and harmony, those who live on the St. Lawrence and the St. John[1] might be expected ordinarily to unite in the choice of a President, with the inhabitants on the banks of the Rio Grande del Norte and the Colorado.[2]

It is evident, at least, that there must be some boundary, or some limits to a republic which is to have a common centre. Free and ardent speculations may lead to the indulgence of an idea that such a republic may be extended over a whole hemisphere. On the other hand, minds less sanguine, or more chastened by the examples of history, may fear that extension often produces weakness, rather than strength; and that political attraction, like other attractions, is less and less powerful, as the parts become more and more distant. In this difference between ardent speculations and cautious fears, it seems to me to be the truest wisdom to abide by the present state of things, since that state of things is acknowledged, on all hands, to be singularly happy, prosperous, and honorable. *In all points of view, therefore, in which I can regard the subject, my judgment is decidedly unfavorable to the project of the annexation of Texas to the United States.* "You have a Sparta"[3] — such was the admonition of the ancient prudence — "embellish it!" We have a republic, gentlemen, of vast extent and unequalled natural advantages; a republic, full of interest in its origin, its history, its present condition, and its prospects for the future. Instead of aiming to enlarge its boundaries, let us seek, rather, to strengthen its union, to draw out its resources, to maintain and improve its institutions of religion and liberty, and thus to push it forward in its career of prosperity and glory.

---

[1] Rivers in the far north of the United States.

[2] Rivers in the Southwest.

[3] An ancient Greek city-state admired in its own day, and in the nineteenth century, because it was relatively free from corruption.

23

JAMES K. POLK

Inaugural Address
March 4, 1845

When Democrat James K. Polk took office as the eleventh president of the United States in 1845, the American public was well aware that he would promote territorial expansion. On the campaign trail, Polk was outspoken in his support of the annexation of both Texas and Oregon, while privately confiding to at least one supporter that he also hoped to take California from Mexico. Whigs (correctly it turns out) warned that Polk would lead the nation to war with Mexico. His election empowered supporters of the annexation of Texas, and a congressional resolution admitting Texas as a state passed on March 1, 1845.

The following passage is taken from Polk's inaugural address. In it he not only states his belief in American exceptionalism and Manifest Destiny, but he also lays claim to both Texas and Oregon. Note how he reiterates Robert J. Walker's claim (see Document 21) that Texas was actually being "reannexed" and how he grounds the U.S. claim on Oregon in America's population growth.

The Republic of Texas has made known her desire to come into our Union, to form a part of our Confederacy and enjoy with us the blessings of liberty secured and guaranteed by our Constitution. Texas was once a part of our country—was unwisely ceded away to a foreign power—is now independent, and possesses an undoubted right to dispose of a part or the whole of her territory and to merge her sovereignty as a separate and independent state in ours. I congratulate my country that by an act of the late Congress of the United States the assent of this Government has been given to the reunion, and it only remains for the two countries to agree upon the terms to consummate an object so important to both.

I regard the question of annexation as belonging exclusively to the United States and Texas. They are independent powers competent to

From James K. Polk, "Inaugural Address," in *A Compilation of the Messages and Papers of the Presidents, 1789–1897*, comp. James D. Richardson (Washington, D.C.: Government Printing Office, 1898), 4:379–81.

contract, and foreign nations have no right to interfere with them or to take exceptions to their reunion. Foreign powers do not seem to appreciate the true character of our Government. Our Union is a confederation of independent States, whose policy is peace with each other and all the world. To enlarge its limits is to extend the dominions of peace over additional territories and increasing millions. The world has nothing to fear from military ambition in our Government. . . . Foreign powers should therefore look on the annexation of Texas to the United States not as the conquest of a nation seeking to extend her dominions by arms and violence, but as the peaceful acquisition of a territory once her own, by adding another member to our confederation, with the consent of that member, thereby diminishing the chances of war and opening to them new and ever-increasing markets for their products.

To Texas the reunion is important, because the strong protecting arm of our Government would be extended over her, and the vast resources of her fertile soil and genial climate would be speedily developed, while the safety of New Orleans and of our whole southwestern frontier against hostile aggression, as well as the interests of the whole Union, would be promoted by it.

In the earlier stages of our national existence the opinion prevailed with some that our system of confederated States could not operate successfully over an extended territory, and serious objections have at different times been made to the enlargement of our boundaries. These objections were earnestly urged when we acquired Louisiana. Experience has shown that they were not well founded. The title of numerous Indian tribes to vast tracts of country has been extinguished; new States have been admitted into the Union; new Territories have been created and our jurisdiction and laws extended over them. As our population has expanded, the Union has been cemented and strengthened. . . . It is confidently believed that our system may be safely extended to the utmost bounds of our territorial limits, and that as it shall be extended the bonds of our Union, so far from being weakened, will become stronger.

. . . I shall . . . endeavor by all constitutional, honorable, and appropriate means to consummate the expressed will of the people and Government of the United States by the reannexation of Texas to our Union at the earliest practicable period.

Nor will it become in a less degree my duty to assert and maintain by all constitutional means the right of the United States to that portion of our territory which lies beyond the Rocky Mountains. Our title to the country of the Oregon is "clear and unquestionable," and already are our people preparing to perfect that title by occupying it with their wives and children. But eighty years ago our population was confined on the west by the ridge of the Alleghanies. Within that period—within the lifetime, I might say, of some of my hearers—our people, increasing to many millions, have filled the eastern valley of the Mississippi, adventurously ascended the Missouri to its headsprings, and are already engaged in establishing the blessings of self-government in valleys of which the rivers flow to the Pacific. The world beholds the peaceful triumphs of the industry of our emigrants. To us belongs the duty of protecting them adequately wherever they may be upon our soil.

24

Uncle Sam's Song to Miss Texas
1845

The popular culture of the day played an important role in advancing the cause of Manifest Destiny. U.S. territorial expansion provided a thrilling theme for artists and writers in the antebellum period. The annexation of Texas, in particular, was widely popular outside New England, and a remarkable outpouring of songs, images, poems, and plays were created in celebration of the event. Although "Uncle Sam's Song to Miss Texas" didn't appear in print until 1848, it likely dates from the period between Polk's election and the start of the U.S.-Mexican War in May 1846. The song, set to the tune of "Yankee Doodle" and thus immediately familiar to listeners, was likely sung both in taverns and by soldiers marching to war in 1846 and 1847.

In Polk's inaugural address (Document 23), he describes the annexation of Texas as an event to be "consummated." Annexation was frequently compared by supporters to a romance or "mixed" marriage between a nonwhite woman (Texas) and a white man (the United States). This song elaborates on the metaphor. Note the racialized and gendered language it employs, revealing the social hierarchy implicit in annexation from the American perspective.

"Uncle Sam's Song to Miss Texas," in *The Rough and Ready Songster* (New York: Nafis and Cornish, 1848), 54–55.

Walk in my tall haired Indian gal,
　　Your hand, my star-eyed Texas,
You're welcome to our White House hall,
　　Tho' Mexy's hounds would vex us;
Come on an' take some Johnny cake,
　　With lasses snug an' coodle,
For that an' Independence make,
　　A full blood Yankee Doodle.
Chorus. — Yankee Doodle is the word,
　　Surpassin' all creation,
With the pipe or with the sword,
　　It makes us love our nation.

My overseer, young Jimmy Polk,
　　Shall show you all my nieces,
An' then the cabinet we'll smoke,
　　Until our eagle sneezes;
If Johnny Bull's[1] fat greedy boys,
　　About our union grumble,
I'll kick up sich a tarnal noise,
　　'Twill make 'em feel quite humble.
　　　　　　　　Yankee Doodle, &c

If Mexy, back'd by secret foes,[2]
　　Still talks of taking you, gal,
Why we can lick 'em all, you know,
　　An' then annex 'em too, gal;
For Freedom's great millenium,
　　Is working airth's salvation,
Her sassy kingdom soon will come,
　　Annexin' all creation.
　　　　　　Singing Yankee Doodle, &c.

[1] A metaphor for Great Britain.
[2] Britain and perhaps France.

25

UNITED STATES DEMOCRATIC REVIEW

Annexation

July–August 1845

The first recorded use of the phrase Manifest Destiny *appeared in the* United States Democratic Review, *a journal affiliated with the Democratic party, in this 1845 article supporting the annexation of Texas. The authorship of this article, like that of "The Great Nation of Futurity" (Document 17), has been contested. Either the editor of the journal, John L. O'Sullivan, or journalist Cora Montgomery (Jane McManus Storm Cazneau) wrote this sweeping vision of America's future on the North American continent.*

"Annexation" not only introduced the term Manifest Destiny *to the public lexicon, but it also offers a classic formulation of American expansionism as natural and inevitable, beneficial to all (except perhaps meddling foreign powers who should have no say in the question), and justified by Anglo-Saxon superiority over other races. The essay also reveals how divisive the issue of slavery was becoming as expansion brought actual and potential slave states into the Union. Although the* Democratic Review *called for national unity over Texas, it is clear that many northerners were far from happy about their new state.*

It is time now for opposition to the Annexation of Texas to cease, all further agitation of the waters of bitterness and strife, at least in connexion with this question—even though it may perhaps be required of us as a necessary condition of the freedom of our institutions, that we must live on for ever in a state of unpausing struggle and excitement upon some subject of party division or other. But, in regard to Texas, enough has now been given to Party. It is time for the common duty of Patriotism to the Country to succeed;—or if this claim will not be recognized, it is at least time for common sense to acquiesce with decent grace in the inevitable and the irrevocable.

From "Annexation," in *United States Magazine and Democratic Review* (Washington, D.C.: Langtree and O'Sullivan, 1845), 17:5, 7, 9.

Texas is now ours. Already, before these words are written, her Convention has undoubtedly ratified the acceptance, by her Congress, of our proffered invitation into the Union; and made the requisite changes in her already republican form of constitution to adopt it to its future federal relations. Her star and her stripe may already be said to have taken their place in the glorious blazon of our common nationality; and the sweep of our eagle's wing already includes within its circuit the wide extent of her fair and fertile land. She is no longer to us a mere geographical space — a certain combination of coast, plain, mountain, valley, forest and stream. She is no longer to us a mere country on the map. She comes within the dear and sacred designation of Our Country; no longer a "*pays*," She is a part of "*la patrie*[1]"; and that which is at once a sentiment and a virtue, Patriotism, already begins to thrill for her too within the national heart. . . .

Why, were other reasoning wanting, in favor of now elevating this question of the reception of Texas into the Union, out of the lower region of our past party dissensions, up to its proper level of a high and broad nationality, it surely is to be found, found abundantly, in the manner in which other nations have undertaken to intrude themselves into it, between us and the proper parties to the case, in a spirit of hostile interference against us, for the avowed object of thwarting our policy and hampering our power, limiting our greatness and checking the fulfilment of our manifest destiny to overspread the continent allotted by Providence for the free development of our yearly multiplying millions. . . .

. . . Mr. Clay[2] was right when he declared that Annexation was a question with which slavery had nothing to do. The country which was the subject of Annexation in this case, from its geographical position and relations, happens to be — or rather the portion of it now actually settled, happens to be — a slave country. But a similar process might have taken place in proximity to a different section of our Union; and indeed there is a great deal of Annexation yet to take place, within the life of the present generation, along the whole line of our northern border. Texas has been absorbed into the Union in the inevitable fulfilment of the general law which is rolling our population westward; the connexion of which with that ratio of growth in population which is destined within a hundred years to swell our numbers to the enormous population of *two hundred and fifty millions* (if not more), is too evident to leave us in

---

[1] From a country to part of "the fatherland," or United States.
[2] Henry Clay, leader of the Whig party and loser in the 1844 presidential election.

doubt of the manifest design of Providence in regard to the occupation of this continent. It was disintegrated from Mexico in the natural course of events, by a process perfectly legitimate on its own part, blameless on ours; and in which all the censures due to wrong, perfidy and folly, rest on Mexico alone. . . .

California will, probably, next fall away from the loose adhesion which, in such a country as Mexico, holds a remote province in a slight equivocal kind of dependence on the metropolis. Imbecile and distracted, Mexico never can exert any real governmental authority over such a country. . . . The Anglo-Saxon foot is already on its borders. Already the advance guard of the irresistible army of Anglo-Saxon emigration has begun to pour down upon it, armed with the plough and the rifle, and marking its trail with schools and colleges, courts and representative halls, mills and meeting-houses. A population will soon be in actual occupation of California, over which it will be idle for Mexico to dream of dominion. They will necessarily become independent. All this without agency of our government, without responsibility of our people—in the natural flow of events, the spontaneous working of principles, and the adaptation of the tendencies and wants of the human race to the elemental circumstances in the midst of which they find themselves placed. . . . Whether they will then attach themselves to our Union or not, is not to be predicted with any certainty. Unless the projected railroad across the continent to the Pacific be carried into effect, perhaps they may not; though even in that case, the day is not distant when the Empires of the Atlantic and Pacific would again flow together into one, as soon as their inland border should approach each other. But that great work, colossal as appears the plan on its first suggestion, cannot remain long unbuilt. Its necessity for this very purpose of binding and holding together in its iron clasp our fast settling Pacific region with that of the Mississippi valley—the natural facility of the route—the ease with which any amount of labor for the construction can be drawn in from the overcrowded populations of Europe, to be paid in the lands made valuable by the progress of the work itself—and its immense utility to the commerce of the world with the whole eastern coast of Asia, alone almost sufficient for the support of such a road—these considerations give assurance that the day cannot be distant which shall witness the conveyance of the representatives from Oregon and California to Washington within less time than a few years ago was devoted to a similar journey by those from Ohio; while the magnetic telegraph will enable the editors of the "San Francisco Union," the "Astoria Evening Post," or the "Nootka Morning News" to set up in type the first half of the President's Inaugural, before the echoes of the latter half shall have died away beneath the lofty porch of the Capitol, as spoken from his lips.

Away, then, with all idle French talk of *balances of power* on the American Continent. There is no growth in Spanish America! Whatever progress of population there may be in the British Canadas, is only for their own early severance of their present colonial relation to the little island three thousand miles across the Atlantic; soon to be followed by Annexation, and destined to swell the still accumulating momentum of our progress.

26

ROBERT WINTHROP

Arbitration of the Oregon Question
January 3, 1846

Whig congressman Robert Winthrop of Massachusetts, like many from his region and party, was deeply ambivalent about annexing territory distant from the center of U.S. political and economic power, particularly if annexation was likely to lead to war. Oregon had been jointly controlled by Great Britain and the United States since 1818, but James K. Polk's supporters, spouting the campaign slogan "Fifty-four forty or fight!," promised to wrestle Oregon from Britain up to 54°40' north latitude. Democratic expansionists frequently threatened to fight anyone who stood in the way of the nation's Manifest Destiny (see Documents 24 and 27).

In January 1846, it looked as if Democrats would make good on their threats against Britain. They proposed to end immediately the joint occupation of Oregon and to raise troops in case Britain refused to renounce its claim to the region. Winthrop spoke out against the bill on the floor of Congress. In the section of his speech reprinted here, he belittles the manhood of Democratic proponents of war and disdainfully mocks the very idea of Manifest Destiny.

From Robert C. Winthrop, "Arbitration of the Oregon Question," in *Addresses and Speeches on Various Occasions* (Boston: Little, Brown, 1852), 483–84, 489–90.

I know that there are those by whom the slightest syllable of dissent from the extreme views which the Administration would seem recently to have adopted, will be eagerly seized upon as evidence of a want of what they call patriotism and American spirit. I spurn all such imputations in advance. I spurn the notion that patriotism can only be manifested by plunging the nation into war, or that the love of one's own country can only be measured by one's hatred to any other country. Sir, the American spirit that is wanted at the present moment, wanted for our highest honor, wanted for our dearest interests, is that which dares to confront the mad impulses of a superficial popular sentiment, and to appeal to the sober second thoughts of moral and intelligent men. Every schoolboy can declaim about honor and war, the British lion and the American eagle; and it is a vice of our nature that the calmest of us have heartstrings which may vibrate for a moment even to such vulgar touches. But,—thanks to the institutions of education and religion which our fathers founded!—the great mass of the American people have, also, an intelligence and a moral sense which will sooner or later respond to appeals of a higher and nobler sort, if we will only have the firmness to make them. . . .

Let me not be misunderstood, Mr. Speaker. I have no hesitation in saying that I honestly think, upon as dispassionate a review of the correspondence as I am capable of, that the American title to Oregon is the best now in existence. But I honestly think, also, that the whole character of the title is too confused and complicated to justify any arbitrary and exclusive assertions of right, and that a compromise of the question is every way consistent with reason, interest, and honor.

There is one element in our title, however, which I confess that I have not named, and to which I may not have done entire justice. I mean that new revelation of right, which has been designated as the right of our manifest destiny to spread over this whole continent. It has been openly avowed, in a leading administration journal,[1] that this, after all, is our best and strongest title; one so clear, so preëminent, and so indisputable, that if Great Britain had all our other titles in addition to her own, they would weigh nothing against it. The right of our manifest destiny! There is a right for a new chapter in the law of nations; or rather in the special laws of our own country; for I suppose the right of a manifest destiny to spread, will not be admitted to exist in any nation except the universal Yankee nation! This right of our manifest destiny, Mr. Speaker, reminds me of another source of title which is worthy of being placed beside

[1] See Document 25.

it. Spain and Portugal, we all know, in the early part of the sixteenth century laid claim to the jurisdiction of this whole northern continent of America. Francis I.[2] is related to have replied to this pretension, that he should like to see the clause in *Adam's Will*, in which their exclusive title was found. Now, Sir, I look for an early reproduction of this idea. I have no doubt that if due search be made, a copy of this primeval instrument, with a clause giving us the whole of Oregon, can be somewhere hunted up. Perhaps it may be found in that same Illinois cave in which the Mormon Testament has been discovered.[3] I commend the subject to the attention of those in that neighborhood, and will promise to withdraw all my opposition to giving notice or taking possession, whenever the right of our manifest destiny can be fortified by the provisions of our great First Parent's last will and testament!

[2] King of France in the early sixteenth century.
[3] Winthrop is referring to the Book of Mormon, derived from texts discovered in New York, not Illinois. The Mormons, a controversial and persecuted new religious sect, were based in Illinois at the time of this speech.

5

War for Empire

27

JAMES K. POLK

Diary Entry

June 30, 1846

President Polk was exceedingly secretive. Although gaining California was one of the main goals of his presidency from the outset, he withheld this information from the American public. After provoking war with Mexico, Polk blamed the conflict on Mexican aggression and claimed that the United States was fighting to restore its honor. Polk remained silent about his desire for Mexican territory in the declaration of war he presented to Congress on May 11, 1846. Nor did he say anything publicly on the subject in the coming months.

Polk kept his territorial ambitions from his cabinet as well. As the following entry in his personal diary makes clear, more than a month into the war, Secretary of State James Buchanan wanted to know "what the objects of the war were." It was only after Buchanan and Secretary of the Treasury Robert J. Walker (see Document 21) argued about how much of Mexico's territory to annex that Polk revealed his ambitions. Buchanan's suggestion was close to the current boundary between Mexico and the United States. Walker's was more expansionistic: A boundary at 26° north latitude would have made the northern third of modern-day Mexico part of the United States. Most of Sonora, Chihuahua, Durango, and Baja California, along with a good portion of Nuevo León and Tamaulipas, would have been U.S. territory. Walker's intransigent response to the European view of this acquisition was typical of southern Democrats and

---

From *The Diary of James K. Polk*, ed. Milo Quaife (Chicago: A. C. McClurg, 1910), 1:495–97.

exactly the kind of bluster that Robert Winthrop critiqued in his January 1846 speech to Congress (Document 26).

   Note how prominent the issue of slavery is in this excerpt and how Buchanan thought the matter of slavery in territories gained from Mexico would be resolved. Note also what those assembled believed about the United States' ability to take Mexican territory at the close of hostilities.

TUESDAY, *30th June, 1846.*—This was the Regular day of meeting of the Cabinet. . . . A discussion arose between Mr. Buchanan and Mr. Walker in regard to the objects of the War against Mexico, in the course of which Mr. Buchanan expressed himself in favour of acquiring the Rio Grande as our Western boundary as high up as the Passo[1] in about latitude 32° of North Latitude & thence West to the Pacific. He expressed himself as being opposed to acquiring any territory by Treaty with Mexico South of 32° of North Latitude. He spoke of the unwillingness of the North to acquire so large a Country that would probably become a slave-holding country if attached to the U.S. Mr. Walker warmly resisted Mr. B.'s views, and insisted that we should if practicable acquire by Treaty, all the country North of a line drawn from the mouth of the Rio Grande in Latitude about 26° West to the Pacific. Mr. Buchanan said it was necessary to know what the objects of the war were, that it might be conducted accordingly; that if it was the object of the President to acquire all the country North of 26°, the line indicated by Mr. Walker, including all of the Department of Tamaulapas, it should be known, and added that if we attempted to acquire all this territory the opinion of the world would be against [us], and especially as it would become a slave-holding country, whereas while it was in possession of Mexico slavery did not exist in it. Mr. Walker remarked that he would be willing to fight the whole world sooner than suffer other Powers to interfere in the matter. I remained silent until the discussion had proceeded to a considerable length, when I spoke, and said in substance that the causes and objects of the war were as I supposed well understood, and that when we came to make peace the terms of the peace would be a subject for consideration. As to the boundary which we should establish by a Treaty of Peace, I remarked that I preferred the 26° to any boundary North of it, but that if it was found that that boundary could not be obtained I was willing to take 32°, but that in any event we must obtain Upper California and New Mexico in any Treaty of Peace we would make. The other

---

[1] El Paso del Norte, or Ciudad Juarez, in Chihuahua, Mexico.

members of the Cabinet expressed no opinions, not being called upon to do so. The discussion between Mr. Buchanan and Mr. Walker was an animated one.

28

JANE SWISSHELM

Protesting the Mexican War
1880

Jane Swisshelm was just twenty-one years old when the United States declared war on Mexico. A deeply religious abolitionist and supporter of woman's rights, she had anonymously written newspaper articles opposed to slavery in her hometown of Pittsburgh. Her opposition to the U.S.-Mexican War, which she viewed as a natural outgrowth of slavery, convinced her to go further, and in 1846 she openly published a series of scathing editorials against the war in a Pittsburgh paper. This was a radical move for a woman at the time. In her 1880 autobiography, she recalled the fierce opposition that drove her to speak out publicly against the war. Like many other Americans, she naturally conflated the war with the extension of slavery. Notice how her sense of religious mission drove her to contest male authority in both her writing and her greeting of Colonel Samuel Black.

In that campaign [the presidential election of 1844], the great Whig argument against the election of Polk was, that it would bring on a war with Mexico for the extension of slavery, and when the war came, Whigs and Liberty Party[1] men vied with each other in their cry of "Our Country, right or wrong!" and rushed into the army over every barrier set up by their late arguments. The nation was seized by a military madness, and in the furore, the cause of the slave went to the wall. . . . It was a dark day for the slave, and it was difficult to see hope for a brighter. To me,

---

[1] The Liberty party was an antislavery third party that endorsed an abolitionist in the presidential elections of 1840 and 1844.

From Jane Grey Swisshelm, *Half a Century* (Chicago: Jansen, McClurg, 1880), 91–96.

it seemed that all was lost, unless some one were especially called to speak that truth, which alone could make the people free, but certainly I could not be the messenger.

For years there had run through my head the words, "Open thy mouth for the dumb, plead the cause of the poor and needy." The streams sang them, the winds shrieked them, and now a trumpet sounded them. . . . If I could "plead the cause" through the press, I must write. . . . No woman had ever done such a thing, and I could never again hold up my head under the burden of shame and disgrace which would be heaped upon me. But what matter? I had no children to dishonor; all save one who had ever loved me were dead, and she no longer needed me, and if the Lord wanted some one to throw into that gulf, no one could be better spared than I. . . .

I do not remember whom I attacked first, but from first to last my articles were as direct and personal as Nathan's reproof to David.[2] . . . This great nation was engaged in the pusillanimous work of beating poor little Mexico—a giant whipping a cripple. Every man who went to the war, or induced others to go, I held as the principal in the whole list of crimes of which slavery was the synonym. Each one seemed to stand before me, his innermost soul laid bare, and his idiosyncrasy I was sure to strike with sarcasm, ridicule solemn denunciations, old truths from [the] Bible and history and the opinions of good men. I had a reckless abandon, for had I not thrown myself into the breach to die there, and would I not sell my life at its full value? . . .

Samuel Black, a son of my pastor, dropped his place as leader of the Pittsburg[h] bar and rushed to the war. My comments were thought severe, even for me, yet the first intimation I had that I had not been cast aside as a monster, came from his sister, who sent me a message that her father, her husband and herself, approved my criticism. Samuel returned with a colonel's commission, and one day I was about to pass him without recognition, where he stood on the pavement talking to two other lawyers, when he stepped before me and held out his hand. I drew back, and he said:

"Is it possible you will not take my hand?"

I looked at it, then into his manly, handsome face, and answered:

"There is blood on it; the blood of women and children slain at their own altars, on their own hearth-stones, that you might spread the glorious American institution of woman-whipping and baby-stealing."

---

[2] Nathan was a prophet who charged David with sinning against God and announced his punishment.

"Oh," he exclaimed, "This is too bad! I swear to you I never killed a woman or a child."

"Then you did not fight in Mexico, did not help to bombard Buena Vista."[3]

His friends joined him, and insisted that I did the Colonel great wrong, when he looked squarely into my face and, holding out his hand, said:

"For sake of the old church, for sake of the old man, for sake of the old times, give me your hand."

I laid it in his, and hurried away, unable to speak, for he was the most eloquent man in Pennsylvania. He fell at last at the head of his regiment, while fighting in the battle of Fair Oaks,[4] for that freedom he had betrayed in Mexico.

[3] Swisshelm is confusing Buena Vista with the Battle of Vera Cruz.
[4] A Civil War battle.

29

GODEY'S LADY'S BOOK

Life on the Rio Grande

April 1847

Godey's Lady's Book, *edited in Philadelphia by Sarah Josepha Hale, was the forerunner of today's women's magazines. It featured sentimental fiction, poetry, articles about fashion and "fashion plates" (full-color etchings of new fashions), and nonfiction stories focusing on women and the home, such as the one excerpted here. At three dollars for a year's subscription, the magazine was quite expensive. But it was also extremely popular among middle-class women, with a circulation in the high five figures in the 1840s.* Godey's *promoted the ideal of the "woman's sphere," or domesticity, which argued that women were especially suited to uplift the family and society through their influence in the home. The magazine avoided political issues and controversial topics, which were considered inappropriate for women. This article about life in Texas, published in the midst of the war between the United States and Mexico, studiously*

From "Life on the Rio Grande," *Godey's Lady's Book*, April 1847, 177.

avoids mentioning the war. But its fawning description of the advance-
ment of civilization in Texas, as well as the improved status of Texas
women, indicates that while domesticity and Manifest Destiny might seem
radically different today, they were actually mutually reinforcing ideolo-
gies. This article suggests that at least some women believed that they had
a crucial role to play in advancing Manifest Destiny.

There they are, pic-nic-ing in real gipsy style, enjoying that life of freedom dwellers in the pent-up city would find so delightful—for a few
days. But the scene will soon be changed. The foot of the Yankee is on
the soil, and his presence is everywhere the harbinger of improvement
and civilization.

It is only eleven years since Texas was a Mexican province, with but
a few thousand of American colonists. It is now a member of the great
family of free states that form the American Union, with more than two
hundred thousand inhabitants. Cities are appearing as by the rubbing
of Aladdin's lamp, dwellings and villages dotting the wide prairies, and
the school-house and church rising side by side, as on our own New
England hills they stand.

As an index of this wonderful change, we saw lately a list of the
post-offices now established in Texas—*one hundred and nineteen!* And
remember, that ten years ago where the greater number of these post-
offices are now located, was wild forest and prairie.

But another and better omen of prosperity is the attention paid to education. It is this feature of life in Texas that gives it a resemblance to the
New England character. As soon as Texas acquired her independence,
she made noble appropriations of land for this object. . . . It seems that
the citizens have now provided free schools for the education of all the
children of Galveston, and this event was one of great rejoicing. They
had a procession, oration, poem, and an evening party, in which parents
and children seem to have been as "happy as happy could be." . . . Men
may enjoy the nomadic life, but for woman the lot is hard. And to show
how highly the influence of the sex is valued in this new state of Texas,
we will quote a few sentences from the eloquent address of General H.
McLeod,[1] delivered at Galveston on the opening of their public schools,
to which we have adverted.

"The civilization of every age has been the reflection of female influence. In the early dispensation she was the handmaid and the hireling,

---

[1] Hugh McLeod, the first Adjutant General of Texas.

and 'when the sound of the grinding was low,' woman still toiled at the mill. Under the grotesque chivalry of the middle ages, she rose from menial servitude to queenly power; from having been man's slave, she became his divinity—she was not loved, but worshiped. The ladye-love of the warrior of the cross was as far from woman's true sphere as were the purchased beauties that filled the harem of his Moslem enemy. Modern enlightenment, with its fearless spirit of investigation, has opened the dawn of a new day, and woman's release from her ancient captivity, has disenthralled mankind.

"Remember then, mothers, that the destiny of your daughters is in your own hands; upon them depend the purity and the virtues of the coming generation. Liberty is ever degenerating into license, and man is prone to abandon his sentiments and follow his passions. It is woman's high mission, her prerogative and duty, to counsel, to sustain—ay, to control him. . . ."

Such are the sentiments of a Texan. If acted upon, and the system of popular education now begun is carried out, that state (or states) will soon be among the brightest lights in our galaxy of stars.

30

WALT WHITMAN

American Workingmen, Versus Slavery

September 1, 1847

Because President Polk was reticent about his war goals (see Document 27), it was far from obvious to most Americans in 1846 that a massive territorial indemnity from Mexico—opening up vast new regions to slavery—would be the result of the conflict. Poet Walt Whitman was one early supporter of the U.S. war against Mexico who was also steadfastly opposed to slavery. As editor of the Brooklyn Daily Eagle *from 1846 to 1848, he predicted, in a piece titled "Shall We Fight It Out?" (May 11, 1846), that a U.S. victory would "teach the world that, while we are not*

From Walt Whitman, "American Workingmen, Versus Slavery," *Brooklyn Daily Eagle*, September 1, 1847, 2.

forward for a quarrel, America knows how to crush, as well as how to expand."

Whitman also warned his urban readers against the increasing power of slavery in American politics. Polk's territorial ambitions became clear on August 8, 1846, when he asked Congress for $2 million to facilitate negotiations with Mexico. The money would be used to pay Mexico for land. Democratic congressman David Wilmot of Pennsylvania offered a proviso to the bill banning slavery from any territory acquired from Mexico. The proviso passed in the House along largely sectional lines but languished in the Senate. Both Polk's war and the proviso greatly exacerbated sectionalism.

In the editorial excerpted here, Whitman frames his support of the Wilmot Proviso in both sectional and class terms, starkly contrasting the interests of the "workingmen," with whom he identified, and slaveowners. Whitman's antislavery views got him fired from the Daily Eagle. *In 1848 he was a delegate to the first national convention of the Free-Soil party, which similarly promoted the notion that slavery degraded free white workers.*

The question whether or no there shall be slavery in the new territories which it seems conceded on all hands we are largely to get through this Mexican war, is a question between *the grand body of white workingmen, the millions of mechanics, farmers, and operatives of our country,* with their interests, on the one side — and the interests of the few thousand rich, "polished," and aristocratic owners of slaves at the south, on the other side. Experience has proved, (and the evidence is to be seen now by any one who will look at it) that a stalwart mass of respectable workingmen, cannot exist, much less flourish, in a thorough slave state. Let any one think for a moment what a different appearance New York, Pennsylvania, or Ohio, would present — how much less sturdy independence and family happiness there would be — were slaves the workmen there, instead of each man as a general thing being his own workman. We wish not at all to sneer at the south; but leaving out of view the educated and refined gentry, and coming to the "common people" of the whites, everybody knows what a miserable, ignorant, and shiftless set of beings they are. Slavery is a good thing enough, (viewed partially,) to the rich — the one out of thousands; but it is destructive to the dignity and independence of all who work, and to labor itself. An honest poor mechanic, in a slave state, is put on a par with the negro slave mechanic—there being many of the latter, who are hired out by their owners. It is of no use to reason abstractly on this fact—farther than to say that the pride of a northern American freeman, poor though he be, will not comfortably stand such degradation. . . .

There can be no half way work in the matter of slavery in the new territory; we must either have it there, or have it not. Now if either the slaves themselves, or their owners, had fought or paid for or gained this new territory, there would be some reason in the pro-slavery claims. But every body knows that the cost and work come, forty-nine fiftieth of it, upon the free man, the middling classes and workingmen, who do their own work and own no slaves. Shall *these* give up all to the aristocratic owners of the south? Will even the poor white free-men of the south be willing to do this? It is monstrous to ask such a thing!

. . . The truth is that . . . the opinions of all our great statesmen . . . are strongly arrayed in favor of limiting slavery to where it already exists. For this the clear eye of Washington looked longingly; for this the great voice of Jefferson plead, and his sacred fingers wrote; for this were uttered the prayers of Franklin and Madison and Monroe. But now, in the south, stands a little band, strong in chivalry, refinement, and genius . . . assuming to speak in behalf of sovereign states, while in real-ity they utter their own idle theories; and disdainfully crying out against the rest of the republic, for whom their contempt is but illy concealed. The courage and high-tone of these men are points in their favor, it must be confessed. With dexterous but brazen logic they profess to stand on the constitution against a principle whose very existence dates from some of the most revered formers of that constitution! And these—this band, really little in numbers, and which could be annihilated by one pulsation of the stout free heart of the north—these are the men who are making such insolent demands, in the face of the working farm-ers and mechanics of the free states—the nine-tenths of the population of the republic. We admire the chivalric bearing (sometimes a sort of impudence) of these men. . . . But the course of moral light and human freedom, (and their consequent happiness,) is not to be stayed by such men as they. Thousands of noble hearts at the north—the entire east—the uprousing giant of the free west—will surely, when the time comes, sweep over them and their doctrines as the advancing ocean tide obliterates the channel of some little brook that erewhile ran down the sands of its shore. Already the roar of the waters is heard; and if a few short sighted ones seek to withstand it, the surge, terrible in its fury, will sweep them too in the ruin.

31

HENRY CLAY

Speech at Lexington, Kentucky
November 13, 1847

Henry Clay, leader of the Whig party, was defeated by James K. Polk in the presidential election of 1844 by the slimmest of margins. In 1846 Whigs begged Clay to speak out against the U.S.-Mexican War, but the three-time presidential candidate, aged and in bad health, instead stayed in seclusion.

In September 1847, General Winfield Scott's troops captured Mexico City, but Mexico refused to negotiate a treaty of peace. In October some expansionists began calling for the annexation of all of Mexico. In November Clay finally agreed to give a public speech about the war. Journalists traveled hundreds of miles to attend this speech, delivered in Clay's hometown of Lexington, Kentucky, and reported in newspapers across the country. Abraham Lincoln, a newly elected U.S. representative from Illinois, was most likely in the audience and adopted many of Clay's views as his own during his single congressional term. Clay spoke out against the spread of slavery. He demanded that the war end immediately, that Mexico keep all of its territory, and that those who shared his views organize in opposition to the war. He also, in the portion of the speech reprinted here, outlined his reasons for opposing the annexation of Mexican territory. Notice how both racism and anti-Catholicism informed Clay's anti-annexation stance.

Shall this War be prosecuted for the purpose of conquering and annexing Mexico, in all its boundless extent, to the United States?

I will not attribute to the President of the United States any such design; but I confess I have been shocked and alarmed by manifestations of it in various quarters. Of all the dangers and misfortunes which could befall this nation, I should regard that of its becoming a warlike and conquering power the most direful and fatal. History tells the mournful tale of conquering nations and conquerors. . . .

Supposing the conquest to be once made, what is to be done with it? Is it to be governed, like Roman Provinces, by Proconsuls? Would it be

From "Mr. Clay's Speech," in David Young, *The Whig Almanac and United States Register for 1848* (New York: Greeley and McElrath, 1847), 22–23.

compatible with the genius, character, and safety of our free institutions, to keep such a great country as Mexico, with a population of not less than nine millions, in a state of constant military subjection?

Shall it be annexed to the United States? Does any considerate man believe it possible that two such immense countries, with territories of nearly equal extent, with populations so incongruous, so different in race, in language, in religion and in laws, could be blended together in one harmonious mass, and happily governed by one common authority? Murmurs, discontent, insurrections, rebellion would inevitably ensue, until the incompatible parts would be broken asunder, and possibly, in the frightful struggle, our present glorious Union itself would be dissevered or dissolved. We ought not to forget the warning voice of all history, which teaches the difficulty of combining and consolidating together conquering and conquered nations. After the lapse of eight hundred years, during which the Moors held their conquest of Spain, the indomitable courage, perseverance and obstinacy of the Spanish race finally triumphed over and expelled the African invaders from the Peninsula. And even within our own time, the colossal power of Napoleon, when at its loftiest hight [sic], was incompetent to subdue and subjugate the proud Castilian. And here in our own neighborhood, Lower Canada, which, near one hundred years ago, after the conclusion of the Seven Years' War, was ceded by France to Great Britain, remains a foreign land in the midst of the British provinces, foreign in feelings and attachment, and foreign in laws, language and religion. And what has been the fact with poor, gallant, generous and oppressed Ireland? Centuries have passed since the overbearing Saxon overran and subdued the Emerald Isle. Rivers of Irish blood have flowed, during the long and arduous contest. Insurrection and rebellion have been the order of the day, and yet, up to this time, Ireland remains alien in feeling, affection and sympathy toward the power which has so long borne her down. Every Irishman hates, with a mortal hatred, his Saxon oppressor. Although there are great territorial differences between the condition of England and Ireland, as compared to that of the United States and Mexico, there are some points of striking resemblance between them. Both the Irish and the Mexicans are probably of the same Celtic race. Both the English and the Americans are of the same Saxon origin. The Catholic Religion predominates in both the former; the Protestant among both the latter. Religion has been the fruitful cause of dissatisfaction and discontent between the Irish and the English nations. Is there no reason to apprehend that it would become so between the people of the United States and those of Mexico, if they were united together?

32

NEW YORK HERALD

Public Meeting in Favor of Annexing All of Mexico
January 30, 1848

Public meetings (similar to today's political rallies) were frequent events in U.S. cities during the 1800s and attracted huge audiences who gathered to hear public figures speak out on issues of importance. They were generally held at night so workingmen could attend and offered one important way for ordinary men to demonstrate their support for expansionism. This meeting, at New York City's Tammany Hall, brought thousands of expansionist Democrats together in support of annexing all of Mexico. Sam Houston, senator from Texas and formally president of the Republic of Texas, was one of several national figures to speak at the meeting. The portion of his speech reprinted here strings together Pilgrims, racism, and sexual fantasy in an astonishing celebration of a hemispheric Manifest Destiny. The New York Herald, *a newspaper that supported the annexation of all of Mexico, reported glowingly on the proceedings.*

THE GREAT WAR MEETING

AT

TAMMANY HALL.

TREMENDOUS GATHERING

OF THE

PEOPLE.

SHALL THE WHOLE OF MEXICO BE

ANNEXED?

THE PRESIDENTIAL RACE

&c. &c. &c.

According to previous notice, at an early hour last evening, the bar room, halls, and stairway of Tammany Hall were crowded. The war question

---

From "The Great War Meeting at Tammany Hall: Tremendous Gathering of the People— Shall the Whole of Mexico Be Annexed?," *New York Herald*, January 30, 1848, 1.

was fully discussed in the bar room, amid brandy and cegar smoke, by those who were waiting for the hall to be opened, that they might be on the spot, to secure a place near the speakers' stand. . . .

At half-past six o'clock, the committee, with the speakers, entered the hall by a private entrance, and took seats on the platform. The doors were then thrown open, and the crowd poured in — some running in one direction, and some in another. In a few moments the room was completely jammed, and a general buzz pervaded. . . .

. . . Calls were now heard, loud and many, for "Houston, Houston." General Samuel Houston, the Texan Senator, and hero of San Jacinto,[1] then stepped forward. His appearance was the signal for loud and deafening cheers; hats were waved, and the thunders of applause were such as almost to shake the foundations of the building. Cries of "hats off," were loud from the crowd behind, anxious to see and hear this much talked of man. After a momentary cessation of the enthusiasm, voices were heard, crying, "Three times three for the Texan hero"; when the roof rang again with reiterated thunders of applauding voices. The tumult of ardent and enthusiastic greeting having stilled, the honorable Senator from Texas addressed the meeting, and said —

Fellow citizens of the Democracy of New York: For the first time in my life I am here presented before an assembly which is the most numerous, the most cheering, and the most emboldening which I ever saw or ever heard of, or ever speculated upon seeing and hearing. . . .

. . . As surely as to-morrow's sun will rise and pursue its bright course along the firmament of heaven, so certain it appears to my mind, must the Anglo Saxon race pervade the whole Southern extremity of this vast continent, and the people whom God has placed here in this land, spread, prevail and pervade throughout the whole rich empire of this great hemisphere. The manner of the consummation of this grand result I cannot predict; but there is an instinct in the American people which impels them onward, which will lead them to pervade this continent, to develope [*sic*] its resources, to civilize its people, and receive the rich bounties of the creating power of the Divine Providence. There is another consideration in this respect, which is conclusive to my mind. The Americans regard this continent as their birth-right. The seed of all their settlements has been sown in blood and watered by blood. The pioneers who went forward into the wilderness poured out their heart's blood to prepare the country for their [posterity]; their scalps were taken by the Indian; they sacrificed their life's blood to acquire the possessions which we enjoy. If all these difficulties and sacrifices did not terrify the bold pioneer, the

---

[1] Key battle in the Texas Revolution.

success of centuries only tends to confirm what they began, and nothing can prevent our mighty march. . . . Your ancestors, when they landed at Plymouth upon that famous rock, were not long contented with that barren spot, but proceeded in their might, and went on progressing at Jamestown as well as at Plymouth, till all the country was possessed by them. From the first moment they landed, they went on trading with the Indians, and cheating them out of their land. Now the Mexicans are no better than Indians, and I see no reason why we should not go on in the same course now, and take their land. . . . Though I am not pious, yet as a sinner I say it, we have a powerful authority for wars in the conduct of the people of Israel, who were led by Divine power to possess themselves of the lands of the Ammonites, and smite them with the edge of the sword. This same mandate from God guides us in this war, and gives success to our army; and I think will continue to guide and to prosper America. I feel grateful for the attention you have given to me; I know I have trespassed upon your time; I would recommend you if the country should be acquired, to take a trip of exploration there, and look out for the beautiful *senoritas*, or pretty girls, and if you should choose to annex them, no doubt the result of this annexation will be a most powerful and delightful evidence of civilization.

33

RAMÓN ALCARAZ ET AL.

Origin of the War with the United States

1848

In the immediate aftermath of the U.S.-Mexican War, a group of fifteen Mexican writers and army officers formed an association to "search for the truth" about the war they had experienced. The volume they produced, modestly titled "Notes for the History of the War between Mexico and the United States," was based on official documents and their firsthand experiences. It appeared in print in Mexico in August 1848, just after the United States ratified the Treaty of Guadalupe Hidalgo, and was

Ramón Alcaraz et al., *The Other Side; or, Notes for the History of the War between Mexico and the United States*, trans. and ed. Albert C. Ramsey (New York: John Wiley, 1850), 1–4, 32.

translated into English by a U.S. Army officer the following year. In the introduction to their history, excerpted here, the authors situate the war within the larger history of U.S. expansionism and pass judgment on Manifest Destiny.

To contemplate the state of degradation and ruin to which the mournful war with the United States has reduced the Republic, is painful. . . . It is to be hoped that the hard lesson which we have received will teach us to reform our conduct; oblige us to adopt the obvious precautions against its repetition; benefit us by being made acquainted with its bitter fruits; induce us not to forget the mistakes we have committed; and prepare us to stay the impending blows with which ambition and treachery threaten us. The Mexican Republic, to whom nature had been prodigal, and full of those elements which make a great and happy nation, had among other misfortunes of less account, the great one of being in the vicinity of a strong and energetic people. Emancipated from the parent country, yet wanting in that experience not to be acquired while the reins of her destiny were in foreign hands, and involved for many years in the whirlwind of never ending revolutions, the country offered an easy conquest to any who might desire to employ against her a respectable force. The disadvantage of her position could not be concealed from the keen sight of the United States, who watched for the favorable moment for their project. For a long time this was carried on secretly, and with caution, until in despair, tearing off the mask, they exposed the plans without disguise of their bold and overbearing policy.

To explain then in a few words the true origin of the war, it is sufficient to say that the insatiable ambition of the United States, favored by our weakness, caused it. But this assertion, however veracious and well founded, requires the confirmation which we will present, along with some former transactions, to the whole world. This evidence will leave no doubt of the correctness of our impressions.

In throwing off the yoke of the mother country, the United States of the North appeared at once as a powerful nation. This was the result of their excellent elementary principles of government established while in colonial subjection. The Republic announced at its birth, that it was called upon to represent an important part in the world of Columbus. Its rapid advancement, its progressive increase, its wonderful territory, the uninterrupted augmentation of its inhabitants, and the formidable power it had gradually acquired, were many proofs of its becoming a colossus, not only for the feeble nations of Spanish America, but even for the old populations of the ancient continent.

The United States did not hope for the assistance of time in their schemes of aggrandizement. From the days of their independence they adopted the project of extending their dominions, and since then, that line of policy has not deviated in the slightest degree. . . .

. . . They desired from the beginning to extend their dominion in such manner as to become the absolute owners of almost all this continent. In two ways they could accomplish their ruling passion: in one by bringing under their laws and authority all America to the Isthmus of Panama; in another, in opening an overland passage to the Pacific Ocean, and making good harbors to facilitate its navigation. By this plan, establishing in some way an easy communication of a few days between both oceans, no nation could compete with them. England herself might show her strength before yielding the field to her fortunate rival, and the mistress of the commercial world might for a while be delayed in touching the point of greatness to which she aspires.

In the short space of some three quarters of a century events have verified the existence of these schemes and their rapid development. The North American Republic has already absorbed territories pertaining to Great Britain, France, Spain, and Mexico. It has employed every means to accomplish this—purchase as well as usurpation, skill as well as force, and nothing has restrained it when treating of territorial acquisition. Louisiana, the Floridas, Oregon, and Texas, have successively fallen into its power. It now has secured the possession of the Californias, New Mexico, and a great part of other States and Territories of the Mexican Republic. Although we may desire to close our eyes with the assurance that these pretensions have now come to an end, and that we may enjoy peace and unmoved tranquillity for a long time, still the past history has an abundance of matter to teach us as yet existing, what has existed, the same schemes of conquest in the United States. The attempt has to be made, and we will see ourselves overwhelmed anew, sooner or later, in another or in more than one disastrous war, until the flag of the stars floats over the last span of territory which it so much covets.

These considerations are indeed mournful; but their certainty can be demonstrated with clearness in proportion to the attention given to their examination. We have observed the constant aim of our neighbor republic. We have fixed upon the period of its independence as a point of interest, after which, as a settled policy, it contemplated this vast dominion. But if we look back upon even earlier times, we will observe that the first settlers of the United States pursued the same ends, and that the descendants of Washington do no more than imitate the conduct of their forefathers.

In truth, subjects of the British throne, whom the religious and political convulsions of their country obliged to seek in distant climes the enjoyment of liberty of conscience and the tranquillity of a peaceful government, established themselves in the territories of North America. Here they did not hesitate to appropriate the possessions of the unhappy natives, that they might change the sickly plant into a vigorous tree with thick foliage and branches, and whose roots would shoot out to a great distance. Then, as now, every method was deemed equally fair; every resource adopted, from the legal purchase of lands, to the taking them by the total extermination of tribes. It is worth noting, however, that in their choice of expedients they preferred those which had the charm of violence. Few indeed followed in the footsteps of the venerable William Penn.[1] . . .

From the acts referred to, it has been demonstrated to the very senses, that the real and effective cause of this war that afflicted us was the spirit of aggrandizement of the United States of the North, availing itself of its power to conquer us. Impartial history will some day illustrate for ever the conduct observed by this Republic against all laws, divine and human, in an age that is called one of light, and which is, notwithstanding, the same as the former—one of *force and violence.*

---

[1] Quaker William Penn, the founder of Pennsylvania, was noted for his good relations with the Leni Lenape (Delaware) inhabitants of the region.

6

Expanded Horizons:
Cuba, Hawaii, and Central America

34

LA VERDAD

Appeal to the Inhabitants of Cuba
April 27, 1848

By 1848 Spain's once mighty New World empire had been reduced to a pair of Caribbean Islands—Cuba and Puerto Rico. Cuba's economy was based on the production of sugar by slave labor and was extremely lucrative for Spain. With its strategic location at the mouth of the Gulf of Mexico, it had long attracted the attention of U.S. expansionists, including Thomas Jefferson, who suggested the expediency of taking Cuba from Spain in a letter to President James Madison in 1809. Spain kept a tight rein on the island, limiting political representation and freedom of the press. By 1848 there were stirrings of independence among some white residents of Cuba, who were inspired by the revolutionary fervor spreading across Europe. To some Americans, after the successful conclusion of the U.S.-Mexican War, Cuba seemed the natural next step in fulfilling America's Manifest Destiny.

Anglo-Americans were joined in this opinion by Cuban émigré communities in New Orleans and New York. They hoped to see Cuba free from Spain's "shackles," and some imagined annexation to the United States a viable option for Cuba. La Verdad *(the* Truth*) was a bilingual newspaper for the Cuban American community published by Cora Montgomery (Jane McManus Storm Cazneau; see Document 35) in New York City in the 1840s and 1850s. Like other Cuban American newspapers of the*

From "Appeal to the Inhabitants of Cuba," *La Verdad*, April 27, 1848.

era, it combined news with political advocacy in favor of Cuban independence. The article excerpted here was reportedly written by a resident of Havana and published there on March 21, 1848. It appeared in Spanish on the front page of La Verdad *on April 27 and was translated into English on an inner sheet of the paper. Notice the reference to "Young America" (see Document 19) and the place of Manifest Destiny in the future freedom of Cuba. Articles like this one helped convince American filibusters that "liberating" Cuba by force was justified.*

Inhabitants of Cuba: A committee of your fellow-citizens address themselves to you on the critical circumstances we are about to meet. Fettered by our barbarous laws, unable to give publicity in this country to our opinions, and deprived of legal means to speak truths that might prevent evils, lead the way to happiness, and make a peaceful revolution, we held in darkness a meeting to deliberate on the saving measures which should be adopted, when, as must inevitably happen, Spain, after the bold example of Republican France, raises the voice of revolution. For the present this is the only medium we find for an appeal—born of our most profound convictions—in the calm voice of reason, to harmonise public opinion, to encourage both the noble and the weak, to intimidate ambitious disorganizers, and lead to a great yet tranquil change in our destiny.

The hour of liberty approaches! At the tremendous echo of the falling thrones of Europe, Republicanism stretches her protecting wings over the earth. Revolution cannot falter in her glorious march which is only opposed by feeble and worn out obstacles, and will overwhelm in her advance the trembling remains of feudalism and monarchy. The severe, upright, and inflexible spirit of the age will make her triumph certain, glorious, and immortal. France in three days overthrew her monarchy; Belgium shakes the throne of her king; Italy moves victorious in all her states, and the magic voice of liberty resounds from her venerated Capitol; Switzerland, relieved from the oppression of the tyrant of France, lifts nobly as ever, her Republican brow. . . . Can Spain rest stationary in the midst of this universal torrent, deaf to the thunder tones of freedom echoing around her? In peace? with such vast evils in her bosom to destroy, such rooted prejudices to extirpate, so many old and deep abuses to reform? Impossible! The oriflamme standard of revolution will sweep over her fields and be planted on the palace of her useless kings, who will share the common fate of their rejected caste. Young America has given the model which proved and perfected by experience, is yet to regenerate Europe, and on this platform will rally the enlightened and convinced nations of the world.

Inhabitants of Cuba! in view of this majestic spectacle, a great danger awaits us if we do not place ourselves in the right channel for the coming torment. . . .

Inhabitants of Cuba, we must not delude ourselves; time presses; we must diffuse light through the masses. The immense majority of the judicious and thinking men of the country, whether of native or foreign birth, think with us. . . . Consider your geographical situation. . . . We are encircled on every side by free American States, destined ere long to be united in one great confederation. How, except in uniting with them, can we assure our pacific revolution, without bloodshed, reactions, hatreds, or retaliations—sufficiently merited and therefore likely to be sufficiently cruel? Consider our internal situation, undermined by diversity of castes, loaded with hatreds born of the injustice of government, with hatreds founded on natural jealousies between Creoles and Peninsulars,[1] and ready to consume the lives and property of all in the volcanic fires which would burst forth if civil discord should [ignite] the blazing torch among us. Assassination, violence, robbery, persecution and anarchy would be the unhappy lot of the pearl of the western seas.

If we have drawn a true picture, if you have hearts, if the divine spark of intelligence illumines your minds, if you desire liberty, peace and the individual security of *all* the inhabitants of this country—safety for yourselves, your interests and your children—weigh these words and propagate this mission of light, liberty and salvation. Away with hatred, forget personal and political offences, the prejudices of nations and of caste and be ready to execute the plan of casting ourselves into the strong, friendly and protecting arms of the Union.

Once more we conjure you; it is our only refuge in this terrible crisis. We cannot resist the revolutionary torrent which agitates the world, it will sweep us on, however reluctant, to independence. In the name of the country we ask of you her salvation, in unity of thought let us all embrace as brothers; let us say "WE WILL IT," with energetic voice, and we will conquer peacefully our liberty and our happiness.

---

[1] Cubans of Spanish descent born in Cuba (creoles) or on the Iberian Peninsula.

35

CORA MONTGOMERY

The Benefits of Annexing Cuba
1850

Jane McManus Storm Cazneau—better known by her pen name, Cora Montgomery—was one of the few female journalists who wrote openly about political topics during the decades before the Civil War. She was also one of the most enthusiastic proponents of Manifest Destiny and, as a writer for the United States Democratic Review, *possibly the author of the phrase itself (see Document 25). Born in Troy, New York, in 1807, she and her father, William McManus, a businessman and veteran of the War of 1812, attempted to establish a settlement in Texas in the early 1830s. She later moved to New York City, where she supported herself as a journalist. Fluent in Spanish, Montgomery traveled throughout the Caribbean and Mexico, including on a government-sponsored secret peace mission to Mexico City in 1846, and lobbied in her writing for the annexation of Nicaragua, Cuba, and the Dominican Republic (a cause her husband, William Cazneau, also championed).*

The essay excerpted here, directed primarily to a northern audience, was published in 1850 not long after a group of Americans under the leadership of Narciso López was expelled from Cuba following an aborted attempt to filibuster the island. Notice the similarities and differences between this appeal and Robert J. Walker's 1844 letter in favor of the "reannexation" of Texas (Document 21), particularly in terms of race and the rise of sectionalism.

Will the Annexation of Cuba Benefit the Domestic Interests of the Union?

Cuba seems placed, by the finger of a kindly Providence, between the Atlantic and the Mexican seas, at the crossing point of all the great lines of our immense coasting trade, to serve as the centre of exchange for a domestic commerce as extensive as our territory, and as free as our

---

From Cora Montgomery, *The Queen of Islands and the King of Rivers* (New York: Charles Wood, 1850), 7, 15–16, 22, 26.

institutions. It is only after a careful study of the incredible extent and variety of the products of our thirty States, with all their grades of climate, and in the whole circumference of their natural and manufactured wealth, and then only with the map of North America distinctly before the eye, that the importance of Cuba, as a point of reception and distribution, can be fairly understood. If her matchless harbors were not locked up by foreign jealousies, and our ships could but find themselves always at home for shelter, water, and refreshment, at this commodious halting place, it would be worth a round purchase sum to our traders, independent of the safe keeping of the Gulf, and the command of her precious staples.

From her central throne she sees our long line of coast break away in numerous links of diverse interests and productions, which must yet intercommunicate past her doors to come to market and value. To the northward she glances along the two thousand miles of seaboard and deep harbors of the "Old Thirteen," all turned toward her to receive her sugar and coffee, and supply her with bread and clothing, even though under the limits and disadvantages of the restrictions of her Spanish masters. . . .

As an open, safe, and reliable haven of rest, aid, and supply, beyond any fear of foreign hostility or interference, standing midway as she does on the path from the Atlantic to the Gulf . . . the control of this Island is of immense, of incomputable importance to the dignity and independence of our coast commerce. It even stands interferingly in the way between the Atlantic ports and the Gulf terminus of the short land route to California, on our own soil, now in course of survey by United States' Engineers, and which a pioneer merchant train of 80 wagons is now traversing under General W. [William] L. Cazneau, with a view to penetrate to the markets of Northern Mexico by the new and direct line from the Gulf. It is the priceless jewel that clasps into one magnificent unbroken chain, the vast circle of our Pacific, Gulf, and Atlantic trade. We only require this one link to belt 5,000 miles of sea-board in close and continuous mart and commercial unity, presenting, on every side, a well connected defence against the pretensions of rival or enemy. Whenever the trembling, restless Seal of the Gulf drops from the nerveless finger of Spain, there will be some envy in Europe, but little open resistance made to its passing into the grasp of our Eagle. When this republic assumes the charge, Europe will retire from this continent, and thenceforth on all our coasts we will ask nothing but our steam marine, and the splendor of our flag, to command the respect of the world for our commerce. . . .

How Will Cuba Influence Slavery?

It is difficult to steer truly and justly between the Scylla and Charybdis of Northern and Southern prejudices, but we may safely aver this much: If England settles the destiny of Cuba, her lot is prefigured in the story of Jamaica, Hayti and Martinico.[1]

If she becomes really independent, the whites, who are but little inferior in numbers to the blacks, will maintain the ascendency by their superior intelligence, and slavery will probably be abolished by slow degrees.

If the United States receive her, humanity will at least rejoice over the suppression of the slave trade, and a mitigation of the horrors of the Spanish system of servitude. . . .

. . . All the territory now held in common — sufficient in area to make forty of the largest States — must inevitably come in free, with or without the interference of Congress, as the climate and character of production will make slave labor unprofitable. To balance this wide domain of free soil, there is but a comparatively small band of States along the extreme South, and to which the Island of Cuba can make no frightful addition.

Our immigration from Europe in a single year amounts to as much as the whole total of the slave inhabitants of Cuba, and after that last fragment of thraldom is brought within the pale of light and freedom, there can be no farther additions. The eighteen millions of whites will enlarge *their* ranks by emigration as well as births, and make stronger every year the disproportion of numbers, but the blacks and African servitude can draw no recruits from abroad. While State after State supplants and drives out unprofitable slave labor by the low wages of sound, mature, and intelligent white industry, hereditary servitude must contract its limits, until it is compressed into those regions of hot, unhealthy marsh in which negroes thrive, but which the constitution of the white man is unequal to the charge of redeeming from jungle and morass — and there slavery will end its mission and depart forever.

The non-slaveholding States would show a most ungenerous sectional spirit if they object to the addition of Cuba to the political weight of the South, for her vote will not give the South an even, much less a controlling voice.

---

[1] Jamaica, Haiti, and Martinique had all abolished slavery by 1850. Montgomery is suggesting that Britain would attempt to abolish slavery in Cuba if it gained control of the island.

36

JAMES BUCHANAN, PIERRE SOULÉ, AND JOHN Y. MASON

The Ostend Manifesto

1854

U.S. presidents continued to press Spain to sell Cuba, even as American filibusters targeted the island. Out of frustration, three of President Franklin Pierce's European diplomats—Pierre Soulé, minister to Spain; James Buchanan, minister to Great Britain; and John Y. Mason, minister to France—met in Ostend, Belgium, in October 1854 to discuss the issue. They penned this memo to Pierce regarding the future of Cuba and the options available to the United States if Spain refused to sell it. Notice the selective reading of America's expansionist past employed by the authors and the relationship drawn here between race and security concerns. Neither the authors of the memo nor Pierce intended for the Ostend Manifesto, as it was known, to become public, but after Soulé revealed details of the meeting, the House of Representatives demanded the document. It was published in the Congressional Globe *in early 1855.*

Considerations exist which render delay in the acquisition of this island exceedingly dangerous to the United States. . . .

It is certain that, should the Cubans themselves organize an insurrection against the Spanish government, and should other independent nations come to the aid of Spain in the contest, no human power could, in our opinion, prevent the people and government of the United States from taking part in such a civil war in support of their neighbors and friends.

But if Spain, dead to the voice of her own interest, and actuated by stubborn pride and a false sense of honor, should refuse to sell Cuba to the United States, then the question will arise, What ought to be the course of the American government under such circumstances? . . .

From Franklin Pierce, "The Ostend Conference, &c.," in *House Executive Documents, 33rd Congress, 2nd Session* No. 93 (Washington, D.C.: Government Printing Office, 1855), 127–32.

The United States have never acquired a foot of territory except by fair purchase, or, as in the case of Texas, upon the free and voluntary application of the people of that independent State, who desired to blend their destinies with our own.

Even our acquisitions from Mexico are no exception to this rule, because, although we might have claimed them by the right of conquest in a just war, yet we purchased them for what was then considered by both parties a full and ample equivalent.

Our past history forbids that we should acquire the island of Cuba without the consent of Spain, unless justified by the great law of self-preservation. We must, in any event, preserve our own conscious rectitude and our own self-respect.

Whilst pursuing this course we can afford to disregard the censures of the world, to which we have been so often and so unjustly exposed.

After we shall have offered Spain a price for Cuba far beyond its present value, and this shall have been refused, it will then be time to consider the question, does Cuba, in the possession of Spain, seriously endanger our internal peace and the existence of our cherished Union?

Should this question be answered in the affirmative, then, by every law, human and divine, we shall be justified in wresting it from Spain if we possess the power; and this upon the very same principle that would justify an individual in tearing down the burning house of his neighbor if there were no other means of preventing the flames from destroying his own home.

Under such circumstances we ought neither to count the cost nor regard the odds which Spain might enlist against us. We forbear to enter into the question, whether the present condition of the island would justify such a measure? We should, however, be recreant to our duty, be unworthy of our gallant forefathers, and commit base treason against our posterity, should we permit Cuba to be Africanized and become a second St. Domingo, with all its attendant horrors to the white race,[1] and suffer the flames to extend to our own neighboring shores, seriously to endanger or actually to consume the fair fabric of our Union.

---

[1] The island of Santo Domingo, or Hispaniola, was divided between French and Spanish rule until 1804, when a series of slave revolts over the previous decade led to the creation of Haiti, the first nation led by blacks in the Western Hemisphere. The idea of a similar slave revolt and an "Africanized" Cuba (an independent nation under black rule) was anathema to slaveholders in the United States.

37

CURRIER AND IVES

The "Ostend Doctrine": Practical Democrats
Carrying Out the Principle
1856

The backlash against the Ostend Manifesto (Document 36) was immediate and severe. European governments protested, Pierre Soulé resigned his post, and Franklin Pierce was forced to abandon his plans for further territorial expansion. This 1856 lithograph, by the preeminent northern printmaking firm Currier and Ives, reflects the views of many in the North that Manifest Destiny in the Caribbean had devolved into highway robbery conducted by and in support of violence-prone slaveholders. It also reflects an anti-immigrant, anti-Catholic bias by portraying the attackers as Irishmen.

In the lithograph, a group of thugs threatens Democrat James Buchanan—one of the manifesto's authors and a candidate for president—using phrases from the document. A ragged Irishman holding a club warns, "If ye don't hand over yer small change in a jiffy ye ould spalpeen 'I'll feel justified' in taking it out of ye wid a touch of this shillaly as 'I pozzis the power.'" Another hoodlum flaunting a large revolver says, "Off with this Coat old fellow! and be quick about it or 'it is not improbable that it may be wrested' from you 'by a successful revolution['] of this six barrel'd joker." Buchanan cries out, "Why! Why! this is rank robbery! Help! Help! all honest men!"

The lithograph, which includes text from the manifesto hanging in the background, was widely reprinted. After the leak of the manifesto, northern support for the annexation of Cuba was extremely limited.

THE "OSTEND DOCTRINE",

Practical Democrats carrying out the principle.

38

T. ROBINSON WARREN

Traveling through the Pacific
1859

T. Robinson Warren was a wealthy New Yorker who, at age twenty-two, joined the exodus to California after gold was discovered there in 1848. He traveled widely throughout the Pacific before returning to New York, getting married, and going to work at the family stockbrokerage. He split his time between stockbroking and writing. His account of his travels, first published in 1858, was one of many travelogues during the decade that extolled the virtues of the independent kingdom of Hawaii, more commonly known as the Sandwich Islands. In the following excerpt, Warren shares his reasons for supporting the annexation of Hawaii. Note how he integrates sex and security concerns into what is essentially a racial argument about "inevitable" annexation.

Lahaina[1] is a stirring little place, straggling along a sand-beach, the romantic little huts half hidden by cocoanut groves, and defended from the foaming surf by a coral reef running along its entire length. Reaching the shore, we find a much larger place than we had supposed, and several prominent buildings, among which were the government house and a Protestant church. There was likewise a pretty good hotel, cosily located, where one could get a fair dinner, and then puff away his cheroot on its balcony, watching the pretty Maui belles as they gracefully tripped along; or, should he prefer it, could swing his hammock beneath the noble cocoas, and snooze away, fanned by the soft trade wind.

The town . . . is embowered in groves of cocoa-nut and bread-fruit, which form long avenues, and beneath whose shade the picturesque cottages are ranged, affording a delightful tropical picture. Around their doors scores of girls were lounging, their beautiful forms enveloped in long, loose gowns, pendant from their shoulders, and their heads

---

[1] Major port town on Maui.

From T. Robinson Warren, *Dust and Foam; or, Three Oceans and Two Continents . . .* (New York: Charles Scribner, 1859), 244–45, 248, 259–61.

surmounted with the jauntiest little glazed hat, with a narrow rim, round the crown of which an ostrich feather tastefully floated.

These girls are grace personified, and the very perfection of physical beauty, and although copper-colored, still that is lost in their full expressive eye and animated features; lolling upon a mat or cane sofa, they would motion you to a seat, when an impromptu flirtation would at once strike up in the most incomprehensible jargon of Kanaka[2] and bad English. However, a squeeze of the hand or a gentle pressure of the waist always elucidates any abstruse remark. . . .

Bidding our Maui friends good bye early one morning, we again got under weigh, and as the sun was setting, found ourselves abreast the Island of Oahu, the queen of the group, and the seat of government, the chief town of which is the city of Honolulu. . . .

Landing, one would fancy himself in a Yankee town, the houses, mostly built of wood, telling of their down-east origin, while their signs, in plain English, testified to the nationality of their owners, and the familiar sounds of Yankee dialect kept up the illusion that we were treading the streets of some Massachusetts seaport, which, however was quickly dispelled by observing names such as Kaaumanu and Nuauanu, painted on sign-boards at the corners of the streets, indicating their designation. Leaving the business part of the town, however, it loses in a measure its Yankee characteristics, and picturesque little cottages, built in a style of their own, embowered in shrubbery, delight the eye. . . .

The fate of the Kanaka like that of the North American Indian, is sealed; he is a doomed man, and it will be but a question of a very few years, when his race will be completely absorbed by the Anglo-Americans. Like the Indian, they fade away before the approach of the white man, not by violence or ill-usage, but the relentless decree of fate, and disease fulfills their inevitable destiny.

During the year 1849–50 the measles, [w]hooping-cough, and influenza, swept off some 9,000 natives; estimating the population at 80,000, this was more than one-eighth of their entire number. Since then, death has been gradually but surely doing its work, with the powerful auxiliaries of syphilis, small pox, and fevers, to so great an extent, that the mortality considerably exceeds the births. From a loose calculation, founded upon facts derived from authentic sources, I should judge that disease, emigration and infanticide, will in less than a century leave these islands without an aboriginal inhabitant.

---

[2] The Hawaiian language; also a native Hawaiian.

Essentially American in feeling and institutions, these islands must, necessarily, eventually fall under the rule of the Americans, in spite of English intrigue, or French bravado,[3] and their importance as an acquisition can scarcely be over estimated.

As an inter-oceanic depot between our western sea-board and the Indies, they are a prime requisite, and no thinking man will doubt, but that the moment the Pacific railroad is definitely fixed upon, schemes of steam navigation will be broached on a scale, such as the world has never dreamed; for with the Chinese ports within forty-five days from our Atlantic sea-board, who will dream of exposing the delicate and costly fabrics of the east to the dangers of a Cape Horn, or Good Hope voyage, not to speak of the immense saving of interest on the capital employed; and such steam communication once established, these islands would of necessity belong to us, for the very population necessary for the transaction of the business and the supply of such an enterprise, would outnumber the present inhabitants of the group, and would of course for their own protection seek admittance into the American Union.

As a naval station it has not its equal; her harbors will accommodate the fleets of the world, and are possessed of natural docks for refitting, and besides are capable of the highest state of defence. With a climate of unprecedented salubrity, and a soil bearing almost spontaneously all the products of temperate and tropic clime, these islands possess advantages for military and naval depots, such a combination of which are not to be found in the world.

---

[3] Both England and France threatened Hawaiian sovereignty in the first half of the nineteenth century.

39

YOUNG SAM

Nicaragua Ho!

January 1856

Filibuster William Walker won great acclaim in the United States after miraculously seizing control of Nicaragua in the fall of 1855. Supporters of Nicaraguan annexation pointed to the precedent of Texas, where a revolution had led to diplomatic recognition by the United States and ultimately annexation. President Franklin Pierce entered office in the late winter of 1853 with grandly expansionistic goals, but controversy over the Ostend Manifesto (see Documents 36 and 37) and respect for the laws of nations tempered any enthusiasm he might otherwise have felt for Walker. Through late 1855 and early 1856, as Pierce refused to recognize Walker's government, the filibuster's supporters became incensed.

Young Sam was a New York newspaper with a humorous bent that was generally opposed to the Pierce administration. Pierce's Nicaraguan policy consumed vast amounts of space in the paper before Walker's fall from power in May 1857. "Nicaragua Ho!" offered lyrics, set to the tune of a popular drinking song, that celebrated the violent, nationalistic "true Americans" who supported Walker. Note at the close of the final stanza the promise of a better life in Nicaragua.

I guess, my Fillibustering pals, that these United States
  of ours,
Tho' pretty large, ain't big enough for all these jolly
  mates of ours.
We ain't got room enough to spread; — our eagle's
  mighty pinions,
Are clipped and fastened to his sides by Pierce and his
  cuss'd minions.
CHORUS — Row, row, row!!!
    My jolly Fillibusters, won't we have a glorious
    row!

From "Nicaragua Ho!," *Young Sam*, January 1856, 67.

It's no use trying to stop us boys when we are on our
    muscle,
With so'thin' or another we are bound to have a tussle;
And, if Marcy[1] thinks the British are too strong, to
    make amends, let's all,
Go and lick the Nicaraguans, who haven't got no
    friends at all.
Row, row, row! &c.

They may issue proclamations for to stop our
    expedition,
But when we go, we shan't request the President's
    permission.
Central America we're bound to take, by gol there's
    nothin' shorter,
And get lots of cash and glory with brave General
    William Walker.
Row, row, row! &c.

Now, spite of Pierce, and John McKeon,[2] and Clayton
    Bulwer treaties,[3]
And tho' cruising in them waters they say a British
    fleet is,
We'll get to Nicaragua yet, thro' all these storms and
    breakers,
And take possession of our Farms and our two
    hundred acres.
Row, row, row! &c.

---

[1] William Marcy, secretary of state under Pierce.

[2] John McKeon, U.S. district attorney for the southern district of New York and enthusiastic prosecutor of filibusters.

[3] The 1850 Clayton-Bulwer Treaty between the United States and Britain specified that neither nation would occupy or colonize any part of Central America.

40

MARTIN DELANY

Political Destiny of the Colored Race on the American Continent

August 24, 1854

The racist assumption that Anglo-Saxons were entitled to take the land of "inferior" nonwhite peoples was central to Manifest Destiny (see Documents 10, 11, 18, 25, 32, 33, and 38). The following document, however, suggests that the appeal of territorial expansion was not limited to white Americans. Martin Delany, an African American abolitionist who was born free in western Virginia in 1812, believed fervently in black nationalism—literally, the founding of a nation where formerly enslaved blacks could forge a homeland free from the discrimination that was universal in the United States.

Some black nationalists looked to Africa for a new home. But at the same time that white expansionists turned their attention to Central America, so too did Delany. In the following excerpt from a speech presented in August 1854 by Delany on behalf of pro-emigration supporters at the National Emigration Convention of Colored People in Cleveland, he outlines the reasons why the Manifest Destiny of African Americans lay in Central America. Notice how his racial and gender beliefs inform his ideas about where to settle. Note, too, Delany's confidence in the continued march of American Manifest Destiny.

Fellow-Countrymen: The duty assigned us is an important one, comprehending all that pertains to our destiny and that of our posterity—present and prospectively. And while it must be admitted that the subject is one of the greatest magnitude, requiring all that talents, prudence and wisdom might adduce, and while it would be folly to pretend to give you the combined result of these three agencies, we shall satisfy ourselves with doing our duty to the best of our ability, and that in the plainest, most simple and comprehensive manner.

From U.S. Congress, House of Representatives, *Report of the Select Committee of Emancipation and Colonization, with an Appendix* (Washington, D.C.: Government Printing Office, 1862), 37, 39–42, 51–52, 59.

Our object, then, shall be to place before you our true position in this country—the United States—the improbability of realizing our desires, and the sure, practicable and infallible remedy for the evils we now endure.

We have not addressed you as *citizens*—a term desired and ever cherished by us—because such you have never been. We have not addressed you as *freemen*—because such privileges have never been enjoyed by any colored man in the United States. Why then should we flatter your credulity, by inducing you to believe that which neither has now, nor never before had an existence. Our oppressors are ever gratified at our manifest satisfaction, especially when that satisfaction is founded upon false premises; an assumption on our part of the enjoyment of rights and privileges which never have been conceded, and which, according to the present system of the United States policy, we never can enjoy. . . .

But we have fully discovered and comprehended the great political disease with which we are affected, the cause of its origin and continuance; and what is now left for us to do is to discover and apply a sovereign remedy—a healing balm to a sorely diseased body—a wrecked but not entirely shattered system. We propose for this disease a remedy. That remedy is emigration. . . .

Several geographical localities have been named, among which rank the Canadas. These we do not object to as places of temporary relief, especially to the fleeing fugitive—which, like a palliative, soothes for the time being the misery—but cannot commend them as permanent places upon which to fix our destiny, and that of our children who shall come after us. . . .

And here we would not deceive you by disguising the facts that, according to political tendency, the Canadas—as all British America— at no very distant day, are destined to come into the United States.

. . . The Yankees from this side of the lakes are fast settling in the Canadas, infusing, with industrious success, all the malignity and negro hate inseparable from their very being, as Christian democrats and American advocates of equality.

Then, to be successful, our attention must be turned in a direction towards those places where the black and colored man comprise, by population, and constitute, by necessity of numbers, the *ruling element* of the body politic, and where, when occasion shall require it, the issue can be made and maintained on this basis; where our political enclosure and national edifice can be reared, established, walled, and proudly defended on this great elementary principle of original identity. Upon this solid foundation rests the fabric of every substantial political structure in the world, which cannot exist without it; and so soon as a people or nation lose their original identity just so soon must that nation or people become extinct. . . .

The truth is, we are not identical with the Anglo-Saxon or any other race of the Caucasian or pure white type of the human family, and the sooner we know and acknowledge this truth the better for ourselves and posterity. . . .

That the colored races have the highest traits of civilization will not be disputed. They are civil, peaceable, and religious to a fault. In mathematics, sculpture, and architecture, as arts and sciences, commerce and internal improvements as enterprises, the white race may probably excel; but in languages, oratory, poetry, music, and painting, as arts and sciences, and in ethics, metaphysics, theology, and legal jurisprudence; in plain language, in the true principles of morals, correctness of thought, religion, and law or civil government, there is no doubt but the black race will yet instruct the world. . . .

We regret the necessity of stating the fact, but duty compels us to the task, that for more than two thousand years the determined aim of the whites has been to crush the colored races wherever found. With a determined will, they have sought and pursued them in every quarter of the globe. The Anglo-Saxon has taken the lead in this work of universal subjugation. But the Anglo-American stands pre-eminent for deeds of injustice and acts of oppression, unparalleled, perhaps, in the annals of modern history. . . .

There is but one question presents itself for our serious consideration, upon which we *must* give a decisive reply: Will we transmit, as an inheritance to our children, the blessings of unrestricted civil liberty, or shall we entail upon them, as our only political legacy, the degradation and oppression left us by our fathers?

Shall we be persuaded that we can live and prosper nowhere but under the authority and power of our North American white oppressors; that this (the United States) is the country most, if not the only one, favorable to our improvement and progress? Are we willing to admit that we are incapable of self-government, establishing for ourselves such political privileges, and making such internal improvements as we delight to enjoy after American white men have made them for themselves?

No! Neither is it true that the United States is the country best adapted to *our* improvement. But that country is the best in which our manhood, morally, mentally, and physically, can be *best developed*; in which we have an untrammelled right to the enjoyment of civil and religious liberty; and the West Indies, Central and South America present now such advantages superiorly preferable to all other countries.

That the continent of America was designed by Providence as a reserved asylum for the various oppressed people of the earth, of all races, to us seems very apparent. . . .

. . . Is it not worthy of a notice here, that while the ingress of foreign whites to this continent has been voluntary and constant, and that of the blacks involuntary and but occasional, yet the whites in the southern part have *decreased* in numbers, *degenerated* in character, and become mentally and physically *enervated* and imbecile; while the blacks and colored people have steadily *increased* in numbers, *regenerated* in character, and have grown mentally and physically vigorous and active, developing every function of their manhood, and are now, in their elementary character, decidedly superior to the white race? So, then, the white race could never successfully occupy the southern portion of the continent; they must, of necessity, every generation, be repeopled from another quarter of the globe. . . .

. . . The West Indians, Central and South Americans, are a noble race of people; generous, sociable and tractable, just the people with whom we desire to unite, who are susceptible of progress, improvement, and reform of every kind. They now desire all the improvements of North America, but being justly jealous of their rights, they have no confidence in the whites of the United States, and consequently peremptorily refuse to permit an indiscriminate settlement among them of this class of people, but placing every confidence in the black and colored people of North America.

The example of the unjust invasion and forcible seizure of a large portion of the territory of Mexico is still fresh in their memory; and the oppressive disfranchisement of a large number of native Mexicans, by the Americans, because of the color and race of the natives, will continue to rankle in the bosom of the people of those countries, and prove a sufficient barrier henceforth against the inroads of North American whites among them.

Upon the American continent, then, we are determined to remain, despite every opposition that may be urged against us. . . .

Now, fellow-countrymen, we have done. Into your ears have we recounted your own sorrows; before your own eyes have we exhibited your wrongs; into your own hands have we committed your own cause. If there should prove a failure to remedy this dreadful evil, to assuage this terrible curse which has come upon us, the fault will be yours and not ours, since we have offered you a healing balm for every sorely aggravated wound.

MARTIN R. DELANY, *Pennsylvania.*
WILLIAM WEBB, *Pennsylvania.*
AUGUSTUS R. GREEN, *Ohio.*
EDWARD BUTLER, *Missouri.*
H. S. DOUGLASS, *Louisiana.*
A. DUDLEY, *Wisconsin.*
CONAWAY BARBOUR, *Kentucky.*
WM. J. FULLER, *Rhode Island.*
WM. LAMBERT, *Michigan.*
J. THEODORE HOLLY, *New York.*
T. A. WHITE, *Indiana.*
JOHN A. WARREN, *Canada.*

41

MARY SEACOLE

A Jamaican's View of Americans in Panama
1857

The gold rushers who traveled through Central America on their way to California in the 1850s behaved badly. Convinced of their racial superiority, frequently calling for the annexation of the region, uninterested in speaking Spanish, and often drunk and disorderly, the mostly young, male crowd that flooded into the cities of Central America did little to endear themselves to the locals. One eyewitness account was offered by Mary Seacole, a mixed-race Jamaican who, in her late forties in 1851, moved to Panama (then part of the Republic of New Granada). She helped her brother run a boardinghouse catering to American travelers during the height of the gold rush. An exceptional woman, Seacole later won fame for her work as a nurse in the Crimean War (1853–1856) and published her autobiography in London in 1857. In the following excerpt from her autobiography, Seacole provides a local perspective on how race and slavery impacted the Central American view of people from the United States.

From Mary Seacole, *Wonderful Adventures of Mrs. Seacole in Many Lands* (London: James Blackwood, 1857), 41, 44–45, 50–52.

Very quarrelsome were the majority of the crowds, holding life cheap, as all bad men strangely do — equally prepared to take or lose it upon the slightest provocation. Few tales of horror in Panama could be questioned on the ground of improbability. Not less partial were many of the natives of Cruces[1] to the use of the knife; preferring, by the way, to administer sly stabs in the back, when no one was by to see the dastard blow dealt. Terribly bullied by the Americans were the boatmen and muleteers, who were reviled, shot, and stabbed by these free and independent filibusters, who would fain whop all creation abroad as they do their slaves at home. . . .

Whenever an American was arrested by the New Granada authorities, justice had a hard struggle for the mastery, and rarely obtained it. Once I was present at the court-house, when an American was brought in heavily ironed, charged with having committed a highway robbery — if I may use the term where there were no roads — on some travellers from Chili [sic]. Around the frightened soldiers swelled an angry crowd of brother Americans, abusing and threatening the authorities in no measured terms, all of them indignant that a nigger should presume to judge one of their countrymen. At last their violence so roused the sleepy alcalde, that he positively threw himself from his hammock, laid down his cigarito, and gave such very determined orders to his soldiers that he succeeded in checking the riot. Then, with an air of decision that puzzled everybody, he addressed the crowd, declaring angrily, that since the Americans came the country had known no peace, that robberies and crimes of every sort had increased, and ending by expressing his determination to make strangers respect the laws of the Republic, and to retain the prisoner; and if found guilty, punish him as he deserved. The Americans seemed too astonished at the audacity of the black man, who dared thus to beard them, to offer any resistance; but I believe that the prisoner was allowed ultimately to escape. . . .

. . . My present life was not agreeable for a woman with the least delicacy or refinement; and of female society I had none. Indeed, the females who crossed my path were about as unpleasant specimens of the fair sex as one could well wish to avoid. With very few exceptions, those who were not bad were very disagreeable, and as the majority came from the Southern States of America, and showed an instinctive repugnance against any one whose countenance claimed for her kindred with their slaves, my position was far from a pleasant one. Not that it ever gave

---

[1] A settlement along the Isthmus route through Panama, midway between the Atlantic and Pacific oceans.

me any annoyance; they were glad of my stores and comforts, I made money out of their wants; nor do I think our bond of connection was ever closer; only this, if any of them came to me sick and suffering (I say this out of simple justice to myself), I forgot everything, except that she was my sister, and that it was my duty to help her.

I may have before said that the citizens of the New Granada Republic had a strong prejudice against all Americans. It is not difficult to assign a cause for this. In the first place, many of the negroes, fugitive from the Southern States, had sought refuge in this and the other States of Central America, where every profession was open to them; and as they were generally superior men—evinced perhaps by their hatred of their old condition and their successful flight—they soon rose to positions of eminence in New Granada. In the priesthood, in the army, in all municipal offices, the self-liberated negroes were invariably found in the foremost rank; and the people, for some reason—perhaps because they recognised in them superior talents for administration—always respected them more than, and preferred them to, their native rulers. So that, influenced naturally by these freed slaves, who bore themselves before their old masters bravely and like men, the New Granada people were strongly prejudiced against the Americans. And in the second and third places, they feared their quarrelsome, bullying habits—be it remembered that the crowds to California were of the lowest sorts, many of whom have since fertilised Cuban and Nicaraguan soil[2]—and dreaded their schemes for annexation. To such an extent was this amusingly carried, that when the American Railway Company took possession of Navy Bay, and christened it Aspinwall, after the name of their Chairman, the native authorities refused to recognise their right to name any portion of the Republic, and pertinaciously returned all letters directed to Aspinwall, with "no such place known" marked upon them in the very spot for which they were intended. And, in addition to this, the legal authorities refused to compel any defendant to appear who was described as of Aspinwall, and put every plaintiff out of court who described himself as residing in that unrecognised place.

Under these circumstances, my readers can easily understand that when any Americans crossed the Isthmus, accompanied by their slaves, the Cruces and Gorgona[3] people were restlessly anxious to whisper into their ears offers of freedom and hints how easy escape would be. Nor were the authorities at all inclined to aid in the recapture of a runaway

---

[2] Seacole is referring to filibusters.
[3] Another stop on the Isthmus route through Panama.

slave. So that, as it was necessary for the losers to go on with the crowd, the fugitive invariably escaped. It is one of the maxims of the New Granada constitution — as it is, I believe, of the English — that on a slave touching its soil his chains fall from him. Rather than irritate so dangerous a neighbour as America, this rule was rarely supported.

7

Sectionalism Trumps Manifest Destiny

42

WILLIAM WALKER

The War in Nicaragua

1860

When Tennessee-born William Walker seized control of Nicaragua in 1855, he became an icon of American Manifest Destiny and a hero across the United States (see Document 39). But once it became clear that President Pierce's administration would not back his regime, Walker looked elsewhere for support. To gain the sympathy of the American South, Walker reintroduced African slavery into Nicaragua in September 1856 even though it had been illegal there for thirty years. Walker was removed from power by a Costa Rican–led army in 1857 and returned to the United States. While workingmen in northern cities still admired his martial virtues, the slavery decree placed Walker firmly on the side of the South in a nation dangerously divided over the issue.

In 1860, on the eve of the Civil War, Walker published an account of his adventures in the hope of gaining financial and political support for a return to the region. In this excerpt, he discusses his controversial slavery decree. Note how he employs Manifest Destiny's racial hierarchy to draw a somewhat radical conclusion about imperialism and the destiny of the South. Walker didn't live long enough to reap the rewards of his publication; he met his death in front of a firing squad in Honduras in 1860 in his final aborted filibuster.

From William Walker, *The War in Nicaragua* (Mobile, Ala.: S. H. Goetzel, 1860), 263, 280, 429–31.

There are many who, while admitting the advantage of slavery to Nicaragua, think it was impolitic to have attempted its re-establishment at the time the decree of the 22d of September was published. This brings us to consider the decree in its relation with the question of slavery in the United States.

. . . The decree, re-establishing slavery while it declared the manner in which the Americans proposed to regenerate Nicaraguan society[,] made them the champions of the Southern States of the Union in the conflict truly styled "irrepressible" between free and slave labor. The policy of the act consisted in pointing out to the Southern States the only means, short of revolution, whereby they can preserve their present social organization. . . .

If there, then, be yet vigor in the South—and who can doubt that there is—for further contest with the soldiers of anti-slavery, let her cast off the lethargy which enthrals her, and prepare anew for the conflict. . . . The true field for the exertion of slavery is in tropical America; there it finds the natural seat of its empire and thither it can spread if it will but make the effort, regardless of conflicts with adverse interests. The way is open and it only requires courage and will to enter the path and reach the goal. Will the South be true to herself in this emergency?

. . . That which you ignorantly call "Filibusterism" is not the offspring of hasty passion or ill-regulated desire; it is the fruit of the sure, unerring instincts which act in accordance with laws as old as the creation. They are but drivellers who speak of establishing fixed relations between the pure white American race, as it exists in the United States, and the mixed Hispano-Indian race, as it exists in Mexico and Central America, without the employment of force. The history of the world presents no such Utopian vision as that of an inferior race yielding meekly and peacefully to the controlling influence of a superior people. Whenever barbarism and civilization, or two distinct forms of civilization, meet face to face, the result must be war. Therefore, the struggle between the old and the new elements in Nicaraguan society was not passing or accidental, but natural and inevitable. The war in Nicaragua was the first clear and distinct issue made between the races inhabiting the northern and the central portions of the continent. But while this contest sprang from natural laws, I trust the foregoing narrative shows that the stronger race kept throughout on the side of right and justice; and if they so maintained their cause in Central America let them not doubt of its future success. Nor kings nor presidents can arrest a movement based on truth and conducted with justice; and the very obstacles they place in the way merely prepare those who are injured for the part they are to play in the world's history. He is but a blind reader of the past who has not learned that Providence fits its agents for great designs by trials, and sufferings, and persecutions. "By the cross thou shalt conquer" is as clearly written in the pages of history as when the startled emperor[1] saw it blazing in letters of light athwart the heavens. In the very difficulties with which the Americans of Nicaragua have had to contend I see the presage of their triumph. Let me, therefore, say to my former comrades, be of good cheer: faint not, nor grow weary by the way, for your toils and your efforts are sure in the end to win success. With us there can be no choice; honor and duty call on us to pursue the path we have entered, and we dare not be deaf to the appeal. By the bones of the mouldering dead at Masaya, at Rivas, and at Granada,[2] I adjure you never to abandon the cause of Nicaragua. Let it be your waking and your sleeping thought to devise means for a return to the land whence we were unjustly brought. And, if we be but true to ourselves, all will yet end well.

[1] Roman emperor Constantine the Great made the cross the Christian standard of war after seeing it in the sky.
[2] Nicaraguan cities where Walker's troops fought.

43

GEORGE SYDNEY HAWKINS

Hostility to Southern Interests
May 31, 1858

The issue of slavery was never separate from that of expansion, but the implications of further territorial acquisition on the sectional balance of slave and free states in the United States became increasingly divisive in the late 1840s. As the North increased in population and power, southerners looked to Mexico, Cuba, and Central America as potential new states where they could expand and maintain slavery. But southern dreams of annexing Cuba, of spreading slavery into Mexico, and of gaining a Central American outpost were repeatedly thwarted. Southerners blamed this on northern hostility to the expansion of slavery.

From "Remarks on the Arrest of William Walker," Cong. Globe, 35th Cong., 1st Sess. (1858), 463.

By the late 1850s, it was not uncommon for southern congressmen to threaten secession and war if northerners continued to block the annexation of new slave territories. Florida representative George Sydney Hawkins concluded a speech on the floor of the House of Representatives in support of filibuster William Walker's right to return to Nicaragua (see Document 42) with the statement excerpted here.

As to the territorial expansion of this country, it is inevitably . . . southward: faster, perhaps, than we wish. You might as well endeavor to prevent the expansion of steam or powder in a state of ignition: but I wish the process fair, and the acquisition gradual. If the people of those countries between the Rio del Norte and the Sierra Madre, irritated to frenzy by constant wars and revolutions, and the perpetual victims of the tyranny of a central power, should achieve their independence and form *de facto* Governments; then, if they should invoke admission into our Union, I say let them come in. Justice and humanity, and the regeneration of a portion of our race would demand this; and let them partake of the benefits of our laws and institutions, our freedom and independence. But if perchance a portion of this Union, guided by a narrow policy and false philanthropy, should oppose such an accession, from hostility to southern interests, a war of opinion may be engendered, and utterance given to it in tones loud and clear as a bugle call; and then, Mr. Chairman, hush who can its irksome echoes!

44

WILLIAM WATERS BOYCE

Why Southerners Should Oppose Territorial Expansion

January 15, 1855

Territorial expansion ground to a halt in the 1850s in large part because northerners and southerners could no longer agree on new targets for annexation. Expansionists in the North looked longingly at Hawaii and Canada; southerners looked to Cuba and other outposts likely to support slavery.

But while many southerners linked the survival of slavery with a Caribbean empire (see Documents 42 and 43), others disavowed territorial expansion. As in the past, many northerners and southerners alike insisted that the nation was large enough and needed to develop its existing resources (see Document 22). Some now believed that territorial expansion was too divisive to continue. By the mid-1850s, an increasing number of states' rights supporters in the South took a different approach. They cautioned against territorial expansion not because it would alienate the North, but because they believed sectional conflict to be inevitable and needed to preserve their resources for the Civil War on the horizon. Congressional debate over the Ostend Manifesto (Document 36) in 1855 provided South Carolina Democrat William Waters Boyce with an opportunity to outline his reasons for opposing territorial acquisition generally, and the acquisition of Cuba specifically.

A feverish impatience seems to be seizing upon our people for territorial extension. In some quarters the cry is for the Canadas. Upon this point, we have been informed by a leading member from Ohio [Mr. CAMPBELL] that the people upon the northern frontier look with deep feeling to the annexation of the British Provinces of North America. In other quarters the cry is for the Sandwich Islands; some are wishing for another

---

From "The Annexation of Cuba: Speech of Hon. W. W. Boyce," *Congressional Globe*, 33rd Cong., 2nd Sess. (1855), 91, 93.

partition of Mexico; others are looking to the regions watered by the mighty Amazon; more are bent upon the acquisition of Cuba, and some have such inordinate stomachs that they are willing to swallow up the entire continent. These are all but various phases of the manifest destiny idea. I must confess, I do not sympathize with this idea. I think our true mission is conservatism, not indefinite extension.

Why do we desire further extension? Do we need any more territory? On the north we lose ourselves upon the verge of eternal snows; on the south we penetrate to the fierce heats of the equator; upon the east and the west we pause only on the beach of the two great oceans of the world. If we apply the instruments we find that the United States are ten times as large as Great Britain, Ireland, and France combined; three times as large as the whole of France, Great Britain, Ireland, Austria, Prussia, Spain, Portugal, Belgium, Holland, and Denmark, nearly equal to the whole of Europe; as large as the Roman Empire when its eagles dominated from the Euphrates to the pillars of Hercules. If it be possible for a nation to have territory enough, we certainly have it, and whatever else we may need, we do not need any more space. If any one were to propose placing the whole of Europe, one of the great divisions of the globe, under a single Government, he would be deemed a madman, yet we realize territorially this idea, and still crave more. What a madness! . . .

Another motive which makes me still more determined not to go to war with Spain for Cuba, is, that we of the South are upon the eve of a great struggle with a hostile majority of the North, and we will need all our resources, not to make foreign conquests, but to defend the very ground upon which we stand. I am, therefore, unwilling to weaken our resources, or complicate our position by an attack on Cuba; others, who hear only the songs of peace in the future, may take a different course.

8

Manifest Destiny Reevaluated and Renewed

45

GEORGE A. CROFUTT

American Progress

ca. 1873

American Progress *is perhaps the preeminent image of Manifest Destiny, but it is a representation suffused with nostalgia. The South lost the Civil War, but Reconstruction and national reunification required sacrifices by both northerners and southerners. The South gave up slavery; the North allowed the South to disenfranchise African Americans and institute a brutal regime of racial oppression.*

Another victim of Reconstruction was historical memory. After the deaths of more than 600,000 Americans in the Civil War, northerners and southerners reimagined the 1840s as a time of shared purpose, when a unified America completed the work of Manifest Destiny and brought progress to the West. In reality, Manifest Destiny was violent and divisive. From the nostalgic perspective of the 1870s, however, it appeared natural and peaceful. In 1872 publisher George A. Crofutt commissioned an image for the frontispiece of the 1874 edition of his western tourist guide, Crofutt's Trans-Continental Tourist Guide. *He asked artist John Gast to illustrate "the grand drama of Progress in the civilization, settlement and history of this country." The resulting image,* American Progress, *so pleased Crofutt that he had a nineteen-color chromolithograph of the image mass-produced and gave a copy to each subscriber to his new magazine,* Crofutt's Western World. *Note how the relative size of the*

George A. Crofutt, *American Progress*, 1873, chromolithograph after an 1872 painting of the same title by John Gast, Prints and Photographs Division, Library of Congress.

figures and the use of light and shadow shape the narrative of this image. Consider why the artist represented "progress" as a woman.

46

SARAH WINNEMUCCA HOPKINS

Trouble on the Paiute Reservation

1865

Although in many ways America's continental expansion was completed with the purchase of Alaska in 1867, Indian peoples still controlled vast portions of the nation's interior. The removal of those peoples to reservations in the late nineteenth century also belongs in the story of Manifest Destiny. Although the United States embraced commercial expansion abroad in this period, within its own boundaries it pursued a relentless course of territorial conquest against Native Americans.

Sarah Winnemucca, born in 1844, was the daughter of a chief of the Paiute (or Piute) tribe in what is now western Nevada. During her lifetime, she witnessed the arrival of white settlers and the repeated mistreatment of the Paiutes at their hands. In the 1880s, she traveled around the United States delivering lectures to raise awareness of her people's plight. Life among the Piutes: Their Wrongs and Claims *(1883) was the first book published in the English language by a Native American woman. The following selection describes the violence that followed the Paiutes onto their reservation in the 1860s.*

This reservation, given in 1860, was at first sixty miles long and fifteen wide. The line is where the railroad now crosses the river, and it takes in two beautiful lakes, one called Pyramid Lake, and the one on the eastern side, Muddy Lake. No white people lived there at the time it was given us. We Piutes have always lived on the river, because out of those two lakes we caught beautiful mountain trout, weighing from two to

---

From Sarah Winnemucca Hopkins, *Life among the Piutes: Their Wrongs and Claims* (Boston: G. P. Putnam's Sons, 1883), 76–78.

twenty-five pounds each, which would give us a good income if we had it all, as at first. Since the railroad ran through in 1867, the white people have taken all the best part of the reservation from us, and one of the lakes also.

The first work that my people did on the reservation was to dig a ditch, to put up a grist-mill and saw-mill. Commencing where the railroad now crosses at Wadsworth, they dug about a mile; but the saw-mill and grist-mill were never seen or heard of by my people, though the printed report in the United States statutes, which my husband found lately in the Boston Athenæum, says twenty-five thousand dollars was appropriated to build them. Where did it go? The report says these mills were sold for the benefit of the Indians who were to be paid in lumber for houses, but no stick of lumber have they ever received. My people do not own any timber land now. The white people are using the ditch which my people made to irrigate their land. This is the way we are treated by our white brothers. Is it that the government is cheated by its own agents who make these reports?

In 1864–5 there was a governor by the name of Nye.[1] There were no whites living on the reservation at that time, and there was not any agent as yet. My people were living there and fishing, as they had always done. Some white men came down from Virginia City to fish. My people went up to Carson City to tell Governor Nye that some white men were fishing on their reservation. He sent down some soldiers to drive them away. Mr. Nye is the only governor who ever helped my people,—I mean that protected them when they called on him in this way.

In 1865 we had another trouble with our white brothers. It was early in the spring, and we were then living at Dayton, Nevada, when a company of soldiers came through the place and stopped and spoke to some of my people, and said, "You have been stealing cattle from the white people at Harney Lake." They said also that they would kill everything that came in their way, men, women, and children. The captain's name was [Almond B.] Wells. The place where they were going to is about three hundred miles away. The days after they left were very sad hours, indeed. Oh, dear readers, these soldiers had gone only sixty miles away to Muddy Lake, where my people were then living and fishing, and doing nothing to any one. The soldiers rode up to their encampment and fired into it, and killed almost all the people that were there.[2] Oh, it

---

[1] James Warren Nye, Nevada's only territorial governor.
[2] Twenty-nine of the thirty people in the encampment were killed by Wells's forces.

is a fearful thing to tell, but it must be told. Yes, it must be told by me. It was all old men, women and children that were killed; for my father had all the young men with him, at the sink of Carson[3] on a hunting excursion, or they would have been killed too. After the soldiers had killed all but some little children and babies still tied up in their baskets, the soldiers took them also, and set the camp on fire and threw them into the flames to see them burn alive. I had one baby brother killed there. My sister jumped on father's best horse and ran away. As she ran, the soldiers ran after her; but, thanks be to the Good Father in the Spiritland, my dear sister got away. This almost killed my poor papa. Yet my people kept peaceful.

That same summer another of my men was killed on the reservation. His name was Truckee John. He was an uncle of mine, and was killed by a man named Flamens, who claimed to have had a brother killed in the war of 1860, but of course that had nothing to do with my uncle. About two weeks after this, two white men were killed over at Walker Lake by some of my people, and of course soldiers were sent for from California, and a great many companies came. They went after my people all over Nevada. Reports were made everywhere throughout the whole country by the white settlers, that the red devils were killing their cattle, and by this lying of the white settlers the trail began which is marked by the blood of my people from hill to hill and from valley to valley.... These reports were only made by those white settlers so that they could sell their grain, which they could not get rid of in any other way. The only way the cattle-men and farmers get to make money is to start an Indian war, so that the troops may come and buy their beef, cattle, horses, and grain. The settlers get fat by it.

[3] Terminus of the Carson River in Nevada.

47

ALBERT J. BEVERIDGE

The March of the Flag

September 16, 1898

In the decades after the Civil War, Americans set aside schemes of annexation and turned to the commercial domination of the globe. From the perspective of 1872 (see Document 45), America's Manifest Destiny was complete with the annexation of California and Oregon in the 1840s.

But perhaps Manifest Destiny was only hibernating in the late nineteenth century. In April 1898, Republican president William McKinley went to war with Spain and gained Cuba, Puerto Rico, and the Philippines. Republicans began to talk again about Manifest Destiny. Albert J. Beveridge, an Indiana lawyer admired for his speaking skills, was a McKinley supporter and champion of an American overseas empire. When Beveridge delivered this speech to the Indiana Republican Campaign in Indianapolis on September 16, 1898, a bloody rebellion was under way in the Philippines, and the status of the territories recently won from Spain was yet to be settled.

Beveridge offers a rousing history of Manifest Destiny and expansionism in his justification for extending colonial rule over American overseas territories. Note the role that trade plays here in legitimating the drive for colonial acquisitions. This celebration of America's new Manifest Destiny was embraced by the Republican party and read at party meetings in Indiana, Iowa, and other states. In 1899 Beveridge was elected to the U.S. Senate from Indiana. He served as a senator for twelve years and much later won acclaim as a Pulitzer Prize–winning historian.

It is a noble land that God has given us; a land that can feed and clothe the world; a land whose coastlines would inclose half the countries of Europe; a land set like a sentinel between the two imperial oceans of the globe, a greater England with a nobler destiny.

From Albert J. Beveridge, "The March of the Flag," in *The Meaning of the Times and Other Speeches* (Indianapolis: Bobbs-Merrill, 1908), 47–52.

It is a mighty people that He has planted on this soil; a people sprung from the most masterful blood of history; a people perpetually revitalized by the virile, man-producing working-folk of all the earth; a people imperial by virtue of their power, by right of their institutions, by authority of their Heaven-directed purposes—the propagandists and not the misers of liberty.

It is a glorious history our God has bestowed upon His chosen people; a history heroic with faith in our mission and our future; a history of statesmen who flung the boundaries of the Republic out into unexplored lands and savage wilderness; a history of soldiers who carried the flag across blazing deserts and through the ranks of hostile mountains, even to the gates of sunset; a history of a multiplying people who overran a continent in half a century; a history of prophets who saw the consequences of evils inherited from the past and of martyrs who died to save us from them; a history divinely logical, in the process of whose tremendous reasoning we find ourselves to-day.

Therefore, in this campaign, the question is larger than a party question. It is an American question. It is a world question. Shall the American people continue their march toward the commercial supremacy of the world? Shall free institutions broaden their blessed reign as the children of liberty wax in strength, until the empire of our principles is established over the hearts of all mankind?

Have we no mission to perform, no duty to discharge to our fellow-man? Has God endowed us with gifts beyond our deserts and marked us as the people of His peculiar favor, merely to rot in our own selfishness, as men and nations must, who take cowardice for their companion and self for their deity—as China has, as India has, as Egypt has?

Shall we be as the man who had one talent and hid it, or as he who had ten talents and used them until they grew to riches? And shall we reap the reward that waits on our discharge of our high duty; shall we occupy new markets for what our farmers raise, our factories make, our merchants sell—aye, and, please God, new markets for what our ships shall carry?

Hawaii is ours; Porto Rico is to be ours; at the prayer of her people Cuba finally will be ours; in the islands of the East, even to the gates of Asia, coaling stations are to be ours at the very least; the flag of a liberal government is to float over the Philippines, and may it be the banner that [General Zachary] Taylor unfurled in Texas and [John C.] Fremont carried to the coast.

The Opposition tells us that we ought not to govern a people without their consent. I answer, The rule of liberty that all just government derives its authority from the consent of the governed, applies only to those who are capable of self-government. We govern the Indians without their consent, we govern our territories without their consent, we govern our children without their consent. How do they know that our government would be without their consent? Would not the people of the Philippines prefer the just, humane, civilizing government of this Republic to the savage, bloody rule of pillage and extortion from which we have rescued them?

And, regardless of this formula of words made only for enlightened, self-governing people, do we owe no duty to the world? Shall we turn these peoples back to the reeking hands from which we have taken them? Shall we abandon them, with Germany, England, Japan, hungering for them? Shall we save them from those nations, to give them a self-rule of tragedy?

They ask us how we shall govern these new possessions. I answer: Out of local conditions and the necessities of the case methods of government will grow. If England can govern foreign lands, so can America. If Germany can govern foreign lands, so can America. If they can supervise protectorates, so can America. Why is it more difficult to administer Hawaii than New Mexico or California? Both had a savage and an alien population; both were more remote from the seat of government when they came under our dominion than the Philippines are to-day.

Will you say by your vote that American ability to govern has decayed; that a century's experience in self-rule has failed of a result? Will you affirm by your vote that you are an infidel to American power and practical sense? Or will you say that ours is the blood of government; ours the heart of dominion; ours the brain and genius of administration? Will you remember that we do but what our fathers did—we but pitch the tents of liberty farther westward, farther southward—we only continue the march of the flag?

The march of the flag! In 1789 the flag of the Republic waved over 4,000,000 souls in thirteen states, and their savage territory which stretched to the Mississippi, to Canada, to the Floridas. The timid minds of that day said that no new territory was needed, and, for the hour, they were right. But [President Thomas] Jefferson, through whose intellect the centuries marched; Jefferson, who dreamed of Cuba as an American state; Jefferson, the first Imperialist of the Republic—Jefferson acquired that imperial territory which swept from the Mississippi to the mountains, from Texas to the British possessions, and the march of the flag began!

The infidels to the gospel of liberty raved, but the flag swept on! The title to that noble land out of which Oregon, Washington, Idaho and Montana have been carved was uncertain; Jefferson, strict constructionist of constitutional power though he was, obeyed the Anglo-Saxon impulse within him, whose watchword then and whose watchword throughout the world to-day is, "Forward!": another empire was added to the Republic, and the march of the flag went on!

Those who deny the power of free institutions to expand urged every argument, and more, that we hear, to-day; but the people's judgment approved the command of their blood, and the march of the flag went on!

A screen of land from New Orleans to Florida shut us from the Gulf, and over this and the Everglade Peninsula waved the saffron flag of Spain; Andrew Jackson seized both, the American people stood at his back, and, under [President James] Monroe, the Floridas came under the dominion of the Republic, and the march of the flag went on! The Cassandras[1] prophesied every prophecy of despair we hear, to-day, but the march of the flag went on!

Then Texas responded to the bugle calls of liberty, and the march of the flag went on! And, at last, we waged war with Mexico, and the flag swept over the southwest, over peerless California, past the Gate of Gold to Oregon on the north, and from ocean to ocean its folds of glory blazed.

And, now, obeying the same voice that Jefferson heard and obeyed, that Jackson heard and obeyed, that Monroe heard and obeyed, that [Secretary of State William] Seward heard and obeyed, that [President Ulysses S.] Grant heard and obeyed, that [President Benjamin] Harrison heard and obeyed, our President to-day plants the flag over the islands of the seas, outposts of commerce, citadels of national security, and the march of the flag goes on! . . .

The ocean does not separate us from lands of our duty and desire—the oceans join us, rivers never to be dredged, canals never to be repaired. Steam joins us; electricity joins us—the very elements are in league with our destiny. Cuba not contiguous! Porto Rico not contiguous! Hawaii and the Philippines not contiguous! The oceans make them contiguous. And our navy will make them contiguous.

. . . We did not need the western Mississippi Valley when we acquired it, nor Florida, nor Texas, nor California, nor the royal provinces of the far northwest. We had no emigrants to people this imperial wilderness,

---

[1] A figure from Greek mythology with the gift of prophecy whom no one believes.

no money to develop it, even no highways to cover it. No trade awaited us in its savage fastnesses. Our productions were not greater than our trade. There was not one reason for the land-lust of our statesmen from Jefferson to Grant, other than the prophet and the Saxon within them. But, to-day, we are raising more than we can consume, making more than we can use. Therefore we must find new markets for our produce.

And so, while we did not need the territory taken during the past century at the time it was acquired, we do need what we have taken in 1898, and we need it now.

A Chronology of Manifest Destiny and American Territorial Expansion (1620–1902)

1620   English Puritans (Pilgrims) land in Plymouth, Massachusetts.

1630   John Winthrop delivers his "citty upon a hill" sermon en route to Massachusetts Bay.

1770–   The white population of the United States doubles to four million;
1790   settlers flood the area west of the Appalachian Mountains.

1785   Congress adopts the Land Ordinance of 1785 to survey land north of the Ohio River and west of the Mississippi; Richard Butler and two other commissioners are sent to negotiate treaties with resident tribes.

1786   *January*   Commissioners negotiate the Treaty of Fort Finney with Shawnee representatives. The treaty is later renounced by the Shawnees.

1787   The Northwest Ordinance provides for the distribution and governance of federal land to the west.

1790–   The white U.S. population more than triples to thirteen million;
1830   conflicts between white settlers and Indian peoples in the Midwest and Southeast increase.

1794   *August 20*   Battle of Fallen Timbers.

1795   *August 2*   Treaty of Greenville; the tribes of the Old Northwest cede land in Ohio and Indiana.

1803   Thomas Jefferson purchases Louisiana from France.

1804–   Meriwether Lewis and William Clark lead an expedition to the
1806   Pacific Northwest.

1811–   *August 1811–January 1812*   Tecumseh travels through the
1812   Southeast and Midwest in an effort to unite Indian peoples against white encroachment.

1812– U.S. attempts to invade Canada and Florida during the War of
1813 1812 fail.

1813 *October 5* Tecumseh killed and his pan-Indian confederacy defeated.

1818 *March* Andrew Jackson invades Spanish Florida.
October Great Britain and the United States agree to joint control of Oregon.

1819 Adams-Onís (Transcontinental) Treaty signed; Spain cedes Florida to the United States and gives up its claim to Oregon; United States gives up its claim to Texas.

1820 The Missouri Compromise prohibits slavery in new territories north of 36°30′ north latitude, with the exception of Missouri.

1823 *December 2* James Monroe presents what will become known as the Monroe Doctrine in his annual message to Congress.

1830 *May 28* Congress passes the Indian Removal Act.

1832 Black Hawk War.

1836 *March 2* Texas declares its independence from Mexico.

1837 *March* The United States recognizes the Republic of Texas.

1838– Cherokees forced west from their Georgia homeland along the
1839 Trail of Tears to Indian Territory (now Oklahoma).

1839 *November* The *United States Democratic Review* publishes "The Great Nation of Futurity."

1840 Richard Henry Dana publishes *Two Years before the Mast.*

1840– Four-and-a-half million immigrants arrive in the United States
1860 from Europe.

1843 A thousand immigrants a year leave Missouri for Oregon along the Overland Trail.

1844 *January* Robert J. Walker publishes his letter in favor of the "reannexation of Texas."

February 7 Ralph Waldo Emerson delivers his "Young American" lecture.

November James K. Polk defeats Henry Clay in the presidential election.

1845 *March 1* Congress passes a joint resolution admitting Texas as a state.

July The *United States Democratic Review* publishes "Annexation."

December 29 Texas becomes the twenty-eighth U.S. state.

1846 *May 11* The United States declares war on Mexico after Polk tells Congress that Mexico has "shed American blood on American soil."

June 15 The United States and Britain sign the Oregon Treaty, establishing a boundary at the forty-ninth parallel.

June 30 Polk admits to his cabinet that he hopes to take all of Mexico north of the twenty-sixth parallel.

August 8 Congressman David Wilmot proposes that slavery be banned from any territory taken from Mexico; the Wilmot Proviso passes in the House but not the Senate.

1846– Brigham Young leads twelve thousand Mormons from the
1847 Midwest to the valley of the Great Salt Lake in Mexico's far northwest.

1847 *September* U.S. forces begin occupying Mexico City.

1847– *October 1847–January 1848* Expansionists call for the
1848 annexation of all of Mexico.

1848 *February 2* The Treaty of Guadalupe Hidalgo ends the U.S.-Mexican War.

1849 Start of the California gold rush; thousands of Americans travel through Central America to reach California; many more travel overland. Narciso López's first unsuccessful invasion of Cuba.

1850 The United States and Britain sign the Clayton-Bulwer Treaty specifying that neither nation will occupy or colonize any part of Central America.

1851 On his third Cuban filibuster, López and his American followers are captured and executed in Cuba. The Treaty of Fort Laramie establishes territories for the Plains tribes.

1852 Franklin Pierce elected president.

1853 *December* The Gadsden Purchase adds 45,535 square miles to the Southwest.

1854 *August 24* Martin Delany delivers his address "Political Destiny of the Colored Race on the American Continent" in Cleveland.

October U.S. diplomats in Belgium sign the Ostend Manifesto.

1855 *Fall* William Walker becomes commander in chief of Nicaragua. Panama Railway completed.

1856 *July* Walker becomes president of Nicaragua; the Pierce administration breaks off relations with the filibuster.

September Walker reinstates African slavery in Nicaragua.

November James Buchanan elected president.

1857 Walker's forces defeated in Nicaragua; he returns to the United States.

1860   Walker executed in Honduras.

1861–
1865   U.S. Civil War.

1867   The United States purchases Alaska from Russia.
        The Kiowas, Comanches, Cheyennes, Arapahos, and Sioux agree
        to move to reservations.

1870   Congress rejects President Ulysses S. Grant's treaty to annex the
        Dominican Republic.

1875   Gold discovered in Deadwood Gulch, on Sioux land.

1876   The U.S. military begins armed actions against the Sioux and
        Cheyennes.

        June 25   Battle of Little Bighorn.

1898   *April–August*   Spanish-American War: the United States annexes
        Hawaii, Guam, the Philippines, and Puerto Rico.

1899–
1902   Philippine-American War.

Questions for Consideration

1. If territorial expansion always involved violently displacing Native Americans from their land, why do we talk about it in terms of land being transferred between European powers and the United States?

2. How did Manifest Destiny evolve from earlier visions of mission and expansion?

3. Was Manifest Destiny anything more than a convenient excuse to steal land? What evidence do we have that people believed in it, and why might they have done so?

4. How was Manifest Destiny gendered?

5. What role did racism play in the ideology and practice of Manifest Destiny? Did Manifest Destiny reflect a distinctly racialized worldview? Did it promote racism?

6. How did Native Americans understand American territorial expansion?

7. How did Mexicans understand American territorial expansion?

8. Did southerners have a different vision of Manifest Destiny than northerners? In what ways were they different, and did their views change over time?

9. Did white men and white women view Manifest Destiny differently?

10. Which Americans believed that it was better to limit the size of the country than to continue expanding? What was their reasoning?

11. Did white Americans differentiate between Mexicans and Indians? Did they believe that one group, or more than one group, had more rights to their land than others?

12. How did anti-Catholicism both promote and inhibit territorial expansion?

13. How and why did ideas of an American empire change dramatically from the 1790s to the 1850s? How did Thomas Jefferson's view of empire differ from that of expansionists in later decades?

14. How was filibustering different from fighting a war? Why was it okay for the United States to declare war on Mexico in order to gain California, but not for William Walker to conquer Nicaragua and call for it to be annexed by the United States?

15. The Ostend Manifesto suggested that the United States was entitled to take Cuba by force if Spain wouldn't sell it. Many Americans who supported the war with Mexico in 1846 opposed the Ostend Manifesto in 1854. Why?

16. Who wanted to annex Cuba? Who was opposed to it? What advantages would the United States gain from annexing Cuba?

17. Why did it make sense for Alaska, but not Nicaragua, to become part of the United States?

18. Was the U.S.-Mexican War a good thing for the United States?

19. Both supporters and opponents of annexing all of Mexico at the close of the U.S.-Mexican War realized that there were millions of people living in central Mexico. Why did opponents of the all-Mexico movement see this as a problem? Why was it okay with supporters?

20. What role did slavery play in the course of Manifest Destiny? How did slavery shape the U.S.-Mexican War? In what ways did it limit territorial expansion in the 1850s?

21. What role did Britain, and fears of Britain, play in advancing territorial expansion?

22. How did territorial expansion exacerbate sectionalism?

23. Why did Manifest Destiny go into eclipse after the Civil War?

24. Why did proponents of territorial expansion, from Richard Butler in 1785 to Albert Beveridge in 1898, talk so much about American history? What did expansionists find so useful about their historically based understanding of American exceptionalism?

25. Do you believe that the United States has a special destiny in the world today?

Selected Bibliography

The following annotated bibliography focuses on classic works on the ideology of Manifest Destiny as well as more recent books that place territorial expansion in its social and cultural contexts, particularly those that explore the experiences of nonwhite peoples.

GENERAL HISTORIES

Anderson, Fred, and Andrew Cayton. *The Dominion of War: Empire and Liberty in North America, 1500–2000.* New York: Viking, 2005. This engaging survey of territorial expansion argues that the United States has always been imperial and has never shied away from using the military to achieve its goals.

Calloway, Colin G. *First Peoples: A Documentary Survey of American Indian History.* 3rd ed. Boston: Bedford/St. Martin's, 2008. The best available textbook covering all of American Indian history. The real strength of this book is the well-chosen documents that follow each chapter. It is also well illustrated.

Cherry, Conrad, ed. *God's New Israel: Religious Interpretations of American Destiny.* Rev. ed. Chapel Hill: University of North Carolina Press, 1998. This collection of lightly edited primary sources with commentary focuses on the theme of American destiny under God and spans the entire course of American history. This is a perfect place to begin reading if you are interested in how a sense of religious mission shaped not just Manifest Destiny but also American reform and social movements.

Drinnon, Richard. *Facing West: The Metaphysics of Indian Hating and Empire Building.* New York: Schocken, 1990. A classic and passionate account of the racism and repression at the heart of U.S. expansionism. Drinnon doesn't mince words and draws a direct line from the policies of Indian extermination in colonial America through the slaughter of the bison on the plains to the Vietnam War.

Hämäläinen, Pekka. *The Comanche Empire.* New Haven, Conn.: Yale University Press, 2008. The author makes a radical argument in favor of viewing the Comanches as the dominant North American empire in the late eighteenth and early nineteenth centuries.

Howe, Daniel Walker. *What Hath God Wrought: The Transformation of America, 1815–1848.* New York: Oxford University Press, 2007. This mammoth narrative history of the Jacksonian era won the Pulitzer Prize for History in 2008. *What Hath God Wrought* covers virtually every aspect of the history of the United States during a time of dramatic change, but it places special emphasis on the importance of territorial expansion during this period. A brilliant synthesis that is especially strong on the political context of the U.S.-Mexican War.

Kaplan, Amy. *The Anarchy of Empire in the Making of U.S. Culture.* Cambridge, Mass.: Harvard University Press, 2002. In six individual case studies, Kaplan charts the significance of ideas of empire in American literary culture, showing how what we now think of as foreign and domestic were closely woven together in the nineteenth century. A challenging read by a literary scholar.

Merk, Frederick. *Manifest Destiny and Mission in American History: A Reinterpretation.* Cambridge, Mass.: Harvard University Press, 1963. A somewhat dated study claiming that Manifest Destiny was a short-lived political movement that died out after the U.S.-Mexican War and rarely captured the imaginations of average Americans.

Slotkin, Richard. *The Fatal Environment: The Myth of the Frontier in the Age of Industrialization, 1800–1890.* Norman: University of Oklahoma Press, 1985. Extremely dense and always thought provoking, this second volume of a trilogy about the American frontier focuses on the archetype of the lone frontiersman/Indian hunter and how it was used to rationalize violence and destruction in the nineteenth century. Weaving together literary texts, newspaper reports, and other cultural artifacts, Slotkin draws breathtaking conclusions.

Stephanson, Anders. *Manifest Destiny: American Expansion and the Empire of the Right.* New York: Hill and Wang, 1995. This brief, opinionated, and entertaining essay on Manifest Destiny from the colonial era to the 1980s focuses primarily on the 1840s and 1890s and suggests that religious motivations were a key component of expansionist ideology. No footnotes.

Weinberg, Albert. *Manifest Destiny: A Study of Nationalist Expansionism in American History.* Chicago: Quadrangle Books, 1963. First published in 1935 by Johns Hopkins University Press. One of the first detailed intellectual histories of the ideology of Manifest Destiny, and in many ways still one of the best. While Weinberg's blind spots about Native Americans, race, and gender are obvious, his command of detail and analysis of how political leaders employed Manifest Destiny as a justification are excellent.

EARLY EXPANSION TO 1830S INDIAN REMOVAL

Aron, Stephen. *How the West Was Lost: The Transformation of Kentucky from Daniel Boone to Henry Clay.* Baltimore: Johns Hopkins University Press,

1996. This study charts the process of settlement in the trans-Appalachian West in the eighteenth and nineteenth centuries. It is particularly enlightening about the roles that land speculation, slavery, and hunting played in the creation of a borderland region.

Onuf, Peter S. *Jefferson's Empire: The Language of American Nationhood.* Charlottesville: University of Virginia Press, 2000. The best work available on the evolution of Thomas Jefferson's ideas of nation and empire.

Owsley, Frank Lawrence, Jr., and Gene A. Smith. *Filibusters and Expansionists: Jeffersonian Manifest Destiny, 1800–1821.* Tuscaloosa: University of Alabama Press, 1997. This study of U.S. foreign policy and expansionism in the South in the early Republic is notable for incorporating Native Americans into the analysis and for the extensive attention it gives to filibusters of the era.

Perdue, Theda, and Michael D. Green. *The Cherokee Removal: A Brief History with Documents.* 2nd ed. Boston: Bedford/St. Martins, 2005. A concise history that explores Indian removal in the 1830s from many different perspectives.

Taylor, Alan. *The Divided Ground: Indians, Settlers, and the Northern Borderland of the American Revolution.* New York: Alfred A. Knopf, 2006. Taylor elegantly charts the struggles of the Iroquois Six Nations of New York and Canada as they attempted to cope with waves of American settlers during and after the American Revolution.

White, Richard. *The Middle Ground: Indians, Empires, and Republics in the Great Lake Region, 1650–1815.* Cambridge, Mass.: Harvard University Press, 1991. This monumental work uncovers a web of mutual accommodation between Algonquians and European settlers in the Great Lakes and Ohio Valley during the century before the American Revolution, and it suggests ways in which American territorial expansion might have proceeded differently.

IDEOLOGY IN THE 1840S

Haynes, Sam W., and Christopher Morris, eds. *Manifest Destiny and Empire: American Antebellum Expansionism.* College Station: Texas A&M University Press, 1997. The fine essays in this collection cover topics central to the political history of Manifest Destiny, including the role of Anglophobia in territorial expansion, filibustering, and the views of U.S. Army officers.

Hietala, Thomas. *Manifest Design: American Exceptionalism and Empire.* Rev. ed. Ithaca, N.Y.: Cornell University Press, 2003. This study of the high politics of territorial expansion makes a strong argument that expansionism in the 1840s was shaped by fears of slavery, freed blacks, and the British, among others, and that Manifest Destiny was deployed by politicians to mask a naked drive for more land and resources for the United States.

Horsman, Reginald. *Race and Manifest Destiny: The Origins of American Racial Anglo-Saxonism.* Cambridge, Mass.: Harvard University Press, 1981. This brilliant intellectual history convincingly grounds Manifest Destiny in the increasing racism of the early nineteenth century.

Hudson, Linda S. *Mistress of Manifest Destiny: A Biography of Jane McManus Storm Cazneau, 1807–1878.* Austin: Texas State Historical Association, 2001. This biography of a little-known female journalist argues that Cazneau, more commonly known as Cora Montgomery, invented the term *Manifest Destiny.*

OREGON, TEXAS, AND MEXICO

DeLay, Brian. *War of a Thousand Deserts: Indian Raids and the U.S.-Mexican War.* New Haven, Conn.: Yale University Press, 2008. This transnational history puts Indian tribes at the center of the conflict over the Southwest between Mexico and the United States. DeLay tells the story of how the interactions and preconceptions of Mexicans, Americans, and independent Indian tribes shaped the borderland region in ways none of the parties expected.

Faragher, John Mack. *Women and Men on the Overland Trail.* Rev. ed. New Haven, Conn.: Yale University Press, 2001. This classic study of the overland journey dispels a number of myths about individualistic western pioneers in its convincing account of family migration to Oregon and California. Faragher looks closely at how and why midwestern families decided to make the long journey west. He also makes excellent use of letters and diaries to explore the day-to-day experiences of women and men on the Overland Trail.

Fuller, John Douglas Pitts. *The Movement for the Acquisition of All Mexico, 1846–1848.* Baltimore: Johns Hopkins Press, 1936. This intensely researched short study argues that support for taking all of Mexico as a spoil of war was quite widespread in the United States before the Treaty of Guadalupe Hidalgo ended the conflict.

Johnson, Susan Lee. *Roaring Camp: The Social World of the California Gold Rush.* New York: W. W. Norton, 2000. This sometimes dense history reveals how multicultural the California gold rush truly was. *Roaring Camp* is especially useful for its examination of the ethnic and class conflict that emerged when Manifest Destiny collided with the wants and desires of Mexican, Chinese, Chilean, French, and African American miners, as well as the Miwok Indian population of the region.

Pletcher, David. *The Diplomacy of Annexation: Texas, Oregon, and the Mexican War.* Columbia: University of Missouri Press, 1973. This meticulous investigation into the diplomatic history of the 1840s clearly reveals the many failures of U.S. diplomacy with Mexico and suggests that with better diplomats, the United States might have avoided war in 1846.

Reséndez, Andrés. *Changing National Identities at the Frontier: Texas and New Mexico, 1800–1850*. New York: Cambridge University Press, 2004. An original study that reveals how fluid identity was in the borderlands during the era of the Texas Revolution and U.S.-Mexican War. It also charts the impact that U.S. economic expansion had in paving the way for annexation.

Robinson, Cecil. *The View from Chapultepec: Mexican Writers on the Mexican-American War.* Tucson: University of Arizona Press, 1989. This is the best translated collection of writings by Mexicans during the U.S.-Mexican War and an excellent source for considering an alternative view of Manifest Destiny.

EXPANSION IN THE 1850S AND SECTIONALISM

Earle, Jonathan H. *Jacksonian Antislavery and the Politics of Free Soil, 1824–1854*. Chapel Hill: University of North Carolina Press, 2004. Earle places conflict over the status of slavery in new territories at the heart of his award-winning study of the rise of early antislavery political parties. Anyone interested in why northerners were so opposed to allowing slavery into new territories, or in the implications of Manifest Destiny on America's political system and the coming of the Civil War, will want to read this book.

Greenberg, Amy S. *Manifest Manhood and the Antebellum American Empire*. New York: Cambridge University Press, 2005. Contrasting aggressive and restrained expansionism, this book argues that a belief in Manifest Destiny was widespread and vibrant in the 1850s and that transformations in gender roles at home drove white men to support war for territory.

Lazo, Rodrigo. *Writing to Cuba: Filibustering and Cuban Exiles in the United States*. Chapel Hill: University of North Carolina Press, 2005. Focusing on previously ignored texts by Cubans and Cuban Americans, Lazo illuminates the meanings of expansionism and Manifest Destiny within Cuban communities in the United States during the nineteenth century.

May, Robert E. *Manifest Destiny's Underworld: Filibustering in Antebellum America*. Chapel Hill: University of North Carolina Press, 2002. In a study full of captivating details, May convincingly argues that support for filibustering was widespread in antebellum America. This is the best work available on filibustering.

McGuinness, Aims. *Path of Empire: Panama and the California Gold Rush*. Ithaca, N.Y.: Cornell University Press, 2008. McGuinness considers the gold rush from the perspective of Panama, which was transformed by the migration of miners through the Isthmus. This is one of the best available works on how Manifest Destiny affected Central Americans.

Morrison, Michael. *Slavery and the American West: The Eclipse of Manifest Destiny and the Coming of the Civil War*. Chapel Hill: University of North Carolina Press, 1997. This detailed and carefully reasoned political history explores the interrelationship between slavery and territorial expansion, showing how conflicts over the expansion of slavery into new territories pushed the United States to civil war in 1861.

EXPANSIONISM AFTER THE CIVIL WAR

Blackhawk, Ned. *Violence over the Land: Indians and Empires in the Early American West*. Cambridge, Mass.: Harvard University Press, 2006. Blackhawk traces the history of conquest and colonialism in the Great Basin (Utah, Nevada, New Mexico, Colorado, and California) across three centuries, focusing in particular on the experiences of the Ute, Paiute, and Shoshone peoples and the extreme violence of American territorial expansion.

Calloway, Colin G., ed. *Our Hearts Fell to the Ground: Plains Indian Views of How the West Was Lost*. Boston: Bedford/St. Martin's, 1996. This short, well-edited collection of Native American views of Manifest Destiny in the late nineteenth and early twentieth centuries includes a concise history of Plains Indian peoples and offers a guide to using Native American sources.

Hoganson, Kristin. *Fighting for American Manhood: How Gender Politics Provoked the Spanish-American and Philippine-American Wars*. New Haven, Conn.: Yale University Press, 1998. Hoganson shows how domestic concerns about effeminacy and racial unrest shaped the drive for war against Spain in 1898.

Isenberg, Andrew C. *The Destruction of the Bison: An Environmental History, 1750–1920*. New York: Cambridge University Press, 2000. This well-organized study of environmental and social change in the Great Plains places Manifest Destiny in a compelling environmental context. Isenberg reveals how changing uses of natural resources on the part of both Native Americans and white settlers interacted with a volatile natural environment, with the result that the Great Plains bison herds were virtually extinct by the early twentieth century. This book is especially strong on the experiences of Plains Indian peoples.

Kramer, Paul. *The Blood of Government: Race, Empire, the United States, and the Philippines*. Chapel Hill: University of North Carolina Press, 2006. Kramer uncovers the racial politics behind the American misadventure in the Philippines in a challenging transnational study that gives equal time to Americans and Filipinos. He shows how empire building transformed ideas of race and nation in both countries.

LaFeber, Walter. *The New Empire: An Interpretation of American Expansionism.* Ithaca, N.Y.: Cornell University Press, 1963. This detailed and clearly argued work of high diplomatic history has aged remarkably well. LaFeber was one of the first to show the role that economic interests played in the imperialism of the 1890s.

Love, Eric T. L. *Race over Empire: Racism and U.S. Imperialism, 1865–1900.* Chapel Hill: University of North Carolina Press, 2004. The provocative thesis of this book is that racism actually inhibited imperialism. Love does an excellent job of charting the twin careers of racism and Manifest Destiny during the decades following the Civil War.

Index

173